Introduction
Understanding the Importance of Conflict Resolution

Conflict is an inherent aspect of human interactions and relationships. It emerges from differing perspectives, varying goals, and diverse personalities. While conflict itself is not inherently negative, how it is managed and resolved can significantly impact the quality of relationships and the overall well-being of individuals and groups. In this chapter, we delve into the fundamental reasons why conflict resolution holds immense importance in our personal, professional, and societal spheres.

The Dynamics of Conflict: A Double-Edged Sword

Conflict can take on various forms, ranging from subtle disagreements to outright clashes. At its core, conflict reflects the diversity of human thoughts, feelings, and desires. While these differences are natural and even beneficial, they can lead to tensions, misunderstandings, and even hostility if not managed appropriately. By understanding the dynamics of conflict, we open the door to constructive resolution that can lead to growth and improved relationships.

Preserving Relationships and Nurturing Growth

In personal relationships, unresolved conflicts can fester and erode the bonds between individuals. Misunderstandings that go unresolved may lead to resentment, communication breakdowns, and emotional distance. Friends, partners, and family members who were once close may drift apart due to lingering tensions. Conflict resolution techniques provide the tools to address these issues head-on, enabling individuals to preserve their connections, rebuild trust, and nurture growth together.

Conflict's Impact on Professional Environments

In professional settings, conflicts can arise from differences in opinions, goals, and workstyles. Unresolved workplace conflicts can lead to decreased morale, decreased productivity, and a toxic work environment. Conversely, when conflicts are managed effectively, they can stimulate creativity, innovation, and improved collaboration. Conflict resolution strategies empower employees and leaders to harness the positive potential of conflicts while mitigating their detrimental effects.

Building a Peaceful Society

On a broader scale, conflict resolution plays a pivotal role in building peaceful societies. Societal conflicts, whether based on cultural, religious, or political differences, can lead to violence, upheaval, and social unrest. Learning to address

Copyright © 2023 by Jonathan T. Morgan (Author)

All rights reserved. No part of this book may be reproduced or utilized in any form or by any means, electronic or mechanical, including photocopying, recording or by any information storage and retrieval system, without permission in writing from the publisher, except for brief quotations in critical articles or reviews.

The content of this book is based on various sources and is intended for educational and entertainment purposes only. While the author has made every effort to ensure the accuracy, completeness, and reliability of the information provided, the information may be subject to errors, omissions, or inaccuracies. Therefore, the author makes no warranties, express or implied, regarding the content of this book.

Readers are advised to seek the guidance of a licensed professional before attempting any techniques or actions outlined in this book. The author is not responsible for any losses, damages, or injuries that may arise from the use of information contained within. The information provided in this book is not intended to be a substitute for professional advice, and readers should not rely solely on the information presented.

By reading this book, readers acknowledge that the author is not providing legal, financial, medical, or professional advice. Any reliance on the information contained in this book is solely at the reader's own risk.

Thank you for selecting this book as a valuable source of knowledge and inspiration. Our aim is to provide you with insights and information that will enrich your understanding and enhance your personal growth. We appreciate your decision to embark on this journey of discovery with us, and we hope that this book will exceed your expectations and leave a lasting impact on your life.

Title: Foundations of Conflict Resolution
Subtitle: Laying the Groundwork for Harmonious Connections

Series: Harmony Within: Mastering Conflict Resolution
Author: Jonathan T. Morgan

Table of Contents

Introduction 5
Understanding the Importance of Conflict Resolution 5
The Impact of Unresolved Conflicts 9
The Path to Harmonious Relationships 13

Chapter 1: Nature of Conflicts 17
Defining Conflicts and Their Varieties 17
Identifying Common Triggers 21
Recognizing the Emotional Dimensions of Conflicts 25
Exploring the Role of Perception in Conflict 29

Chapter 2: Effective Communication 33
The Role of Communication in Conflict Resolution 33
Active Listening Techniques 38
The Power of Non-Verbal Communication 42
Constructive Expression of Thoughts and Feelings 47

Chapter 3: Self-Awareness in Conflict 52
Unveiling Your Triggers and Reactions 52
Cultivating Emotional Intelligence 56
The Art of Self-Reflection 61
Mindfulness Practices for Conflict Resolution 66

Chapter 4: Empathy and Perspective-Taking 71
The Importance of Empathy in Resolving Conflicts 71
Practicing Perspective-Taking 76
Building Bridges through Empathetic Communication 81
Empathy's Role in Reducing Misunderstandings 86

Chapter 5: De-Escalation Techniques 92

Understanding Escalation and Its Dangers 92

Strategies for Preventing Conflict Escalation 97

Diffusing Tensions through Calmness and Understanding .. 102

Stepping Back to Find Clarity and Solutions 107

Chapter 6: Effective Problem Solving 113

Identifying the Underlying Issues in Conflicts 113

Brainstorming Solutions Collaboratively 117

Prioritizing and Evaluating Potential Solutions 122

Implementing and Reviewing Conflict Resolution Strategies 127

Chapter 7: Empowerment through Boundaries 132

The Role of Boundaries in Conflict Prevention 132

Setting and Communicating Personal Boundaries 138

Respecting Others' Boundaries 143

Finding Balance between Flexibility and Boundaries 148

Conclusion 155

Reflecting on Your Conflict Resolution Journey 155

Applying Foundational Principles in Real-Life Situations ... 160

The Ongoing Path to Mastering Conflict Resolution 166

Wordbook 172

Supplementary Materials 176

these conflicts through peaceful means is essential for maintaining stability and promoting the well-being of all members of society. Conflict resolution equips communities and nations with the tools to engage in dialogue, negotiate, and find common ground.

Conflict as a Catalyst for Personal Growth

When approached with the right mindset, conflict can serve as a catalyst for personal growth and self-awareness. By navigating conflicts, individuals are forced to confront their own biases, triggers, and limitations. This process of self-reflection and growth not only enhances their ability to resolve conflicts constructively but also contributes to their overall emotional intelligence and resilience.

The Ripple Effect: From Individual to Global Impact

Every conflict resolved positively has a ripple effect that extends beyond the immediate parties involved. When individuals learn to address conflicts without resorting to aggression or avoidance, they model effective communication and problem-solving for others. This creates a culture of understanding and cooperation that can permeate families, workplaces, communities, and even global interactions.

In the following chapters, we will explore the foundational principles of conflict resolution in greater detail. From effective communication to empathy and problem-solving techniques, these tools will empower you to transform conflicts into opportunities for growth and understanding. By understanding the pivotal role conflict resolution plays in our lives, we embark on a journey toward healthier relationships, enhanced personal development, and a more harmonious world.

The Impact of Unresolved Conflicts

Conflict is an ever-present force in human relationships and interactions. While it can be a catalyst for growth and change, unresolved conflicts have the potential to leave lasting scars on individuals, relationships, and even entire communities. In this chapter, we delve into the profound and often overlooked consequences of allowing conflicts to fester without resolution, exploring the wide-reaching effects that can reverberate through personal, interpersonal, and societal levels.

The Quiet Erosion of Trust and Connection

When conflicts remain unresolved, trust erodes over time. Whether it's between spouses, friends, colleagues, or nations, the failure to address differences and misunderstandings can lead to a breakdown in trust. Individuals become hesitant to communicate openly or share vulnerabilities, fearing that their concerns will be dismissed or lead to further conflict. This erosion of trust seeps into the foundation of relationships, weakening their resilience and inhibiting emotional intimacy.

Communication Breakdowns and Emotional Toll

Unresolved conflicts often give rise to communication breakdowns. When people avoid discussing the issues at hand, they inadvertently create an environment where misunderstandings thrive. As emotions intensify, rational discussions become increasingly challenging, replaced by heated arguments or cold silence. The emotional toll of such conflicts can be immense, leading to stress, anxiety, and even depression as individuals grapple with the weight of unresolved issues.

The Proliferation of Misunderstandings

One of the most insidious impacts of unresolved conflicts is the proliferation of misunderstandings. Minor disagreements can snowball into major issues when left unaddressed. As assumptions and interpretations take center stage, the original cause of the conflict may become obscured. These misunderstandings can lead to a vicious cycle of recurring conflicts, further deepening the divide between parties.

A Stifling Environment for Growth

In personal relationships and professional settings alike, unresolved conflicts create an environment that stifles growth. Individuals and teams become focused on managing the tensions rather than pursuing productive goals. Creativity, innovation, and collaboration suffer as attention shifts from shared objectives to managing interpersonal tensions. The energy required to navigate unresolved conflicts drains resources that could be better invested in personal development and shared success.

Escalation and the Domino Effect

Left unchecked, conflicts can escalate, leading to a domino effect that affects multiple aspects of life. A minor disagreement between partners, for instance, can lead to increased stress at home, diminished focus at work, and strained relationships with friends and family. The ripple effect of unresolved conflicts can disrupt multiple areas of one's life, leading to a cycle of negativity that is difficult to break.

A Catalyst for Social Instability

On a larger scale, unresolved conflicts have the potential to fuel social instability and even violence. Societal tensions that are not addressed can erupt into protests, uprisings, or even armed conflicts. In the absence of constructive resolution mechanisms, resentment festers, and individuals may resort to extreme measures to express their grievances. The impact of these conflicts extends beyond the individuals directly involved, affecting entire communities and regions.

The Quest for Resolution and Healing

Understanding the far-reaching consequences of unresolved conflicts underscores the urgency of addressing them. It highlights the importance of fostering a culture of open communication, empathy, and proactive conflict resolution. By acknowledging the impact of unresolved conflicts, we are motivated to seek healthier ways to engage with differences and find common ground.

As we journey through the following chapters, we will equip ourselves with the tools and strategies to navigate conflicts constructively. By understanding the gravity of unresolved conflicts, we pave the way for healing, growth, and the cultivation of harmonious relationships at all levels of our lives.

The Path to Harmonious Relationships

At the heart of conflict resolution lies the aspiration for harmonious relationships. While conflicts are inevitable in human interactions, the way we navigate and resolve them shapes the quality of our connections and the overall well-being of our lives. In this chapter, we embark on a journey to explore the essential principles that guide us toward building and sustaining harmonious relationships through effective conflict resolution.

Cultivating Open Dialogue: A Cornerstone of Connection

Central to the path of harmonious relationships is the cultivation of open dialogue. When we engage in honest and respectful conversations, we create a safe space for sharing thoughts, feelings, and concerns. Open dialogue fosters understanding and empathy, helping individuals see beyond their differences and explore common ground. By communicating openly, we lay the foundation for resolving conflicts in a manner that respects each person's perspective.

Empathy: Bridging the Gap Between Minds and Hearts

Empathy serves as a bridge that connects minds and hearts, transcending the boundaries of personal experiences. When we put ourselves in others' shoes, we gain insights into their feelings, motivations, and aspirations. This deep understanding forms the basis for compassionate communication and constructive conflict resolution. Empathy helps us move from a mindset of confrontation to one of collaboration, where we work together to find solutions that honor the needs of all parties involved.

From "Me" to "We": Embracing a Collaborative Mindset

Shifting from a "me" perspective to a "we" perspective is essential for building harmonious relationships. This change in mindset acknowledges that conflicts involve multiple perspectives and that resolutions should benefit all parties. Collaborative conflict resolution involves brainstorming solutions, listening to differing viewpoints, and jointly identifying strategies that satisfy everyone's needs. This approach fosters a sense of shared ownership over the resolution process and promotes a deeper sense of unity.

The Power of Forgiveness and Letting Go

Harboring resentment and holding onto grudges can impede the path to harmonious relationships. Forgiveness is not about condoning hurtful actions, but rather about releasing the emotional burden that comes with holding onto anger and pain. Letting go of the past allows space for healing and growth, enabling individuals to move forward with an open heart and a willingness to rebuild trust.

Setting Boundaries: The Art of Self-Care and Respect

Boundaries play a crucial role in maintaining harmonious relationships. When individuals clearly define and communicate their personal boundaries, they express their needs and limits. Respecting others' boundaries demonstrates empathy and consideration. Striking a balance between flexibility and boundaries ensures that relationships are built on mutual respect, where each person's well-being is honored.

The Continuous Cycle of Learning and Improvement

The path to harmonious relationships is not a destination but a continuous journey of learning and improvement. As we encounter conflicts and navigate resolutions, we refine our communication skills, deepen our empathy, and enhance our problem-solving abilities. Each conflict presents an opportunity for growth, allowing us to become more attuned to the nuances of human interaction and better equipped to build stronger connections.

Creating a Ripple of Positive Change

The pursuit of harmonious relationships through conflict resolution carries the potential for positive change that extends far beyond individual connections. By modeling effective conflict resolution in our interactions, we inspire others to adopt similar approaches. As harmonious relationships ripple outward, they contribute to the creation of more compassionate communities, healthier workplaces, and a more harmonious world.

In the forthcoming chapters, we will delve into the practical techniques and strategies that empower us to walk the path of harmonious relationships. From effective communication to empathy and problem-solving, these tools will guide us toward resolving conflicts constructively and nurturing connections that stand the test of time. By embracing these principles, we embark on a transformative journey that enriches our lives and the lives of those around us.

Chapter 1: Nature of Conflicts
Defining Conflicts and Their Varieties

Conflict, in its myriad forms, is an integral part of the human experience. It arises from the diversity of perspectives, needs, and desires that characterize our interactions. In this chapter, we delve into the foundational aspects of conflicts, exploring their definitions, sources, and the various types that shape our lives.

The Essence of Conflict: A Clash of Perspectives

At its core, conflict can be defined as a clash of perspectives, interests, or goals between individuals or groups. It emerges when differing viewpoints collide, leading to tension, disagreement, and, in some cases, emotional turmoil. Conflict is not inherently negative; it is a natural outcome of human diversity. However, the way conflicts are managed and resolved plays a critical role in determining their impact on relationships.

Sources of Conflict: Triggers and Underlying Issues

Conflicts can stem from a variety of sources, ranging from external triggers to underlying issues that have been brewing beneath the surface. External triggers might include differences in opinion, values, or priorities. These triggers bring existing tensions to the forefront. However, conflicts often have deeper roots, such as unmet needs, unresolved past issues, or miscommunication. Identifying these underlying sources is crucial for addressing conflicts at their core.

Varieties of Conflict: From Subtle to Overt

Conflicts come in various shades, ranging from subtle disagreements to overt clashes. Some conflicts are more overt, characterized by open disagreements and heated arguments. Others are more subtle, manifesting as passive-aggressive behavior or a lack of cooperation. Conflicts can also be latent, lying dormant until triggered by specific events or circumstances. Recognizing these different manifestations helps us tailor our conflict resolution approaches accordingly.

Interpersonal Conflicts: Relationships Under Pressure

Interpersonal conflicts occur between individuals who share a relationship. These conflicts can emerge in friendships, romantic partnerships, family relationships, or professional connections. Interpersonal conflicts often stem from personal differences, unmet expectations, and communication breakdowns. Effectively addressing these conflicts requires empathy, active listening, and a willingness to understand each party's perspective.

Intrapersonal Conflicts: The Battle Within

Intrapersonal conflicts occur within an individual's mind and heart. These conflicts might involve conflicting emotions, desires, or values. For example, an individual might experience inner conflict when trying to balance personal ambitions with family responsibilities. Self-awareness and introspection play a significant role in resolving intrapersonal conflicts, as individuals must navigate their own thoughts and feelings to find resolution.

Inter-group and Societal Conflicts: A Wider Lens

Conflicts can also extend beyond individual relationships to encompass groups or entire societies. These conflicts might emerge from cultural differences, historical grievances, or systemic inequalities. Inter-group and societal conflicts are complex and often require multi-faceted approaches that address deep-rooted issues. Effective resolution involves understanding the historical context, promoting dialogue, and working toward social change.

Managing Conflict: A Lifelong Skill

Understanding the diverse forms of conflicts provides a foundation for effective resolution. By recognizing the triggers, sources, and varieties of conflicts, we equip ourselves with the tools to navigate them constructively. As we journey through this book, we will delve deeper into the techniques and strategies that empower us to address conflicts in ways that promote understanding, empathy, and ultimately, the path to harmonious relationships.

Identifying Common Triggers

Conflicts, as intricate and diverse as they may be, often arise from common triggers that ignite differences and tensions between individuals or groups. In this chapter, we delve into the core triggers that frequently give rise to conflicts, exploring the psychological, emotional, and situational factors that contribute to their emergence. By understanding these triggers, we can cultivate greater awareness and proactive strategies to address conflicts constructively.

Miscommunication and Misunderstandings: Seeds of Conflict

One of the most prevalent triggers of conflicts is miscommunication. Misunderstandings can stem from vague language, differing interpretations, or assumptions about intentions. A simple statement can be misconstrued, leading to confusion, hurt feelings, and escalating tensions. Recognizing the potential for miscommunication empowers individuals to be more vigilant in clarifying their thoughts and intentions, reducing the likelihood of conflicts arising from misunderstandings.

Unmet Needs and Expectations: Fuel for Discontent

Unmet needs and unfulfilled expectations often serve as potent triggers for conflicts. In personal relationships, individuals might feel neglected or undervalued when their emotional needs are not acknowledged. In professional settings, unmet expectations regarding roles, responsibilities, or career growth can lead to frustration and resentment. Identifying these triggers requires honest self-assessment and open communication to bridge the gap between expectations and reality.

Differences in Values and Beliefs: A Clash of Perspectives

Conflicts often stem from differences in values, beliefs, and worldviews. When individuals hold contrasting moral, cultural, or religious beliefs, clashes can occur, especially in diverse social or work environments. Acknowledging these differences and approaching them with empathy is crucial for preventing conflicts and fostering understanding. Constructive dialogue that allows individuals to share their viewpoints and learn from one another can lead to mutual respect rather than animosity.

Competing Interests and Scarce Resources: The Battle for Gain

Competing interests and limited resources can ignite conflicts, as individuals or groups vie for a share of the pie. Whether it's a disagreement over a promotion at work, a dispute over shared property, or a clash over budget allocation within an organization, conflicts can arise when parties perceive that their interests are at odds. Balancing the needs and desires of all parties involved while seeking win-win solutions can defuse these triggers and promote cooperation.

Change and Uncertainty: Navigating the Unknown

Change, whether anticipated or unexpected, can trigger conflicts as individuals adjust to new circumstances. People often resist change due to fear of the unknown, the potential loss of comfort, or the challenge of adapting to new norms. Conflicts can arise when individuals are resistant to change or when changes disrupt established routines. Communicating the rationale behind changes and involving affected parties in decision-making can mitigate these triggers.

Power Imbalances and Hierarchies: Struggles for Control

Power dynamics can be powerful triggers of conflicts, particularly in relationships with imbalanced power structures. Whether it's a boss-employee relationship, a parent-child dynamic, or a situation involving social hierarchies, conflicts can arise when one party perceives a lack of control or autonomy. Addressing power imbalances through open dialogue and empowerment strategies can alleviate tensions and lead to more equitable relationships.

Cultural and Identity Differences: Navigating Diversity

In culturally diverse societies, conflicts often arise from differences in identities, backgrounds, and traditions. Cultural misunderstandings, stereotypes, and biases can fuel tensions and escalate conflicts. Embracing cultural sensitivity, learning about other cultures, and engaging in open conversations can bridge gaps and promote harmonious interactions.

Harnessing Awareness for Conflict Resolution

Identifying common triggers empowers individuals to anticipate and address conflicts before they escalate. By recognizing the sources of tension and implementing proactive strategies, individuals can prevent conflicts from taking root or escalating to harmful levels. The journey toward effective conflict resolution begins with this heightened awareness, laying the groundwork for the techniques and tools we'll explore in the chapters ahead.

Recognizing the Emotional Dimensions of Conflicts

Conflict is not solely a battle of words or ideas; it is deeply intertwined with human emotions. Emotions play a pivotal role in shaping the nature, intensity, and resolution of conflicts. In this chapter, we delve into the emotional dimensions of conflicts, exploring how emotions drive conflicts, influence behavior, and impact the potential for resolution. Understanding these emotional aspects is essential for navigating conflicts effectively and fostering harmonious relationships.

The Role of Emotions in Conflict: Fueling the Fire

Emotions serve as the fuel that ignites conflicts and propels them forward. When individuals feel hurt, frustrated, or threatened, these emotions can drive them to engage in defensive or aggressive behaviors. Recognizing and acknowledging these emotional triggers is crucial for addressing conflicts at their source and preventing them from escalating further.

Fear and Insecurity: Underlying Motivations

Fear and insecurity often lurk beneath the surface of conflicts. Individuals may fear loss, rejection, or the unknown, prompting defensive reactions that perpetuate conflicts. Insecurity can lead to a desire for control or validation, which can clash with the desires and needs of others. By understanding these underlying emotional motivations, we gain insight into the root causes of conflicts and can approach resolutions with greater empathy.

Anger and Frustration: The Explosive Catalysts

Anger and frustration are potent emotional catalysts that can intensify conflicts. When individuals feel their needs are unmet or their values are disregarded, anger can surface as a protective mechanism. Unchecked anger, however, can lead to destructive confrontations. Recognizing the signs of anger and learning techniques for managing it constructively is essential for de-escalating conflicts and fostering productive communication.

Hurt and Resentment: Lingering Emotions

Past hurts and unresolved resentments often contribute to ongoing conflicts. Individuals may carry emotional baggage from previous interactions, causing them to react defensively even in unrelated situations. Recognizing and addressing these lingering emotions is essential for breaking the cycle of conflict and creating a space for healing and reconciliation.

Empathy and Compassion: Bridges to Resolution

On the other side of the emotional spectrum, empathy and compassion hold the power to bridge divides and foster resolutions. When individuals empathize with each other's emotions and experiences, they establish a connection that transcends differences. Empathy opens the door to effective communication, as parties are more likely to listen and collaborate when they feel understood and valued.

Emotional Contagion: The Ripple Effect

Emotions are contagious, and their impact extends beyond the immediate parties involved in a conflict. Negative emotions can spread through social networks, influencing perceptions and fueling further conflicts. On the flip side, positive emotions, such as empathy and understanding, can also spread, contributing to a culture of constructive conflict resolution and cooperation.

Emotional Regulation: A Key Skill for Resolution

Recognizing the emotional dimensions of conflicts underscores the importance of emotional regulation. Developing the ability to manage one's own emotions and respond to others' emotions effectively is essential for navigating conflicts constructively. Techniques such as deep breathing, mindfulness, and reframing can help individuals maintain emotional balance and approach conflicts with a clear and level-headed mindset.

Empowering Conflict Resolution through Emotional Intelligence

Emotional intelligence—the capacity to understand and manage one's emotions and the emotions of others—is a cornerstone of effective conflict resolution. By honing emotional intelligence skills, individuals can navigate conflicts with empathy, self-awareness, and interpersonal effectiveness. These skills enhance communication, de-escalate tensions, and pave the way for collaborative solutions.

From Emotional Awareness to Resolution

Recognizing the emotional dimensions of conflicts equips individuals with a deeper understanding of the forces at play. Emotions drive conflicts, but they also hold the potential for resolution. By approaching conflicts with emotional awareness, empathy, and emotional intelligence, we transform conflicts from destructive battles into opportunities for growth, understanding, and the cultivation of harmonious relationships.

Exploring the Role of Perception in Conflict

Perception, the lens through which we interpret the world around us, plays a profound role in shaping conflicts. Two individuals can witness the same event yet perceive it entirely differently, leading to disagreements and misunderstandings. In this chapter, we delve into the intricate role of perception in conflicts, understanding how our cognitive biases, past experiences, and personal filters influence the way we perceive situations and interact with others. By unraveling the complexities of perception, we can gain insights into conflict dynamics and work toward more effective resolutions.

Perception as a Filter: Shaping Our Reality

Perception serves as a filter through which we process information and construct our reality. Our perceptions are influenced by a multitude of factors, including cultural background, upbringing, personal experiences, and emotional state. As a result, what one person perceives as a harmless comment, another might interpret as a slight. Understanding that everyone sees the world through their unique perceptual lens is a crucial step toward empathy and conflict resolution.

Cognitive Biases: The Unseen Influencers

Cognitive biases are inherent mental shortcuts that affect how we perceive and interpret information. These biases can lead us to jump to conclusions, make assumptions, or overlook evidence that contradicts our preconceived notions. Confirmation bias, for instance, causes us to seek out information that confirms our existing beliefs while ignoring contradictory evidence. Becoming aware of cognitive biases allows us to approach conflicts with a more open and rational mindset.

Selective Attention: What We See and Ignore

Selective attention refers to our tendency to focus on certain aspects of a situation while ignoring others. In conflicts, this can lead to individuals fixating on negative details and disregarding positive ones. For example, during an argument, one party might remember only the hurtful words spoken rather than the attempts at understanding. Recognizing the role of selective attention helps us uncover hidden dimensions of conflicts and facilitates more balanced perspectives.

Attribution Theory: Assigning Causes to Behaviors

Attribution theory explores how we assign causes to behaviors, whether they are our own or others'. When conflicts arise, we often attribute negative motives to the actions of others while attributing our own actions to external circumstances. This bias can escalate conflicts by fueling resentment and misunderstanding. Becoming aware of attribution tendencies enables us to question our assumptions and consider alternative explanations for behaviors.

Past Experiences and Emotional Baggage: Shaping Perceptions

Past experiences and emotional baggage significantly influence the way we perceive conflicts. If someone has been hurt in a similar situation before, they might approach a current conflict with heightened defensiveness. Unresolved past conflicts can color our perceptions, leading to misunderstandings and preventing us from engaging in constructive dialogue. Addressing emotional baggage through self-awareness and communication can pave the way for more objective perceptions.

Empathy and Perspective-Taking: Expanding Perceptions

Empathy and perspective-taking are powerful tools for broadening our perceptions. When we step into someone else's shoes and view a situation from their perspective, we gain insights into their thoughts, feelings, and motivations. This expanded perception fosters understanding and reduces the tendency to jump to conclusions. Practicing empathy enables us to approach conflicts with a willingness to see beyond our own vantage point.

Conflict Resolution through Perception Management

Understanding the role of perception in conflicts offers a path to more effective resolution. By recognizing our own biases, challenging assumptions, and embracing empathy, we can manage our perceptions to navigate conflicts constructively. This involves actively seeking alternative viewpoints, engaging in open dialogue, and reframing situations to uncover shared interests. Perception management empowers individuals to dismantle barriers to understanding and collaborate toward solutions.

The Quest for Objective Understanding

While complete objectivity might be elusive due to the inherent subjectivity of perception, striving for a more balanced and informed understanding is essential. Engaging in introspection, seeking diverse perspectives, and being open to adjusting our viewpoints when presented with new information are critical steps toward achieving a clearer perception. As we explore the intricacies of perception, we unlock the potential to transform conflicts into opportunities for growth, empathy, and harmonious relationships.

Chapter 2: Effective Communication

The Role of Communication in Conflict Resolution

Communication serves as the linchpin of conflict resolution. It's the vehicle through which individuals express their thoughts, feelings, and concerns, and it lays the groundwork for understanding and collaboration. In this chapter, we delve into the critical role that communication plays in resolving conflicts, exploring how effective communication techniques can dismantle barriers, promote empathy, and pave the way for productive resolutions.

The Foundation of Understanding: Effective Communication

Effective communication is the foundation upon which conflict resolution is built. Clear and open communication allows individuals to express their perspectives, needs, and emotions, facilitating a deeper understanding of the issues at hand. By actively engaging in communication, parties involved in conflicts create a platform for dialogue that goes beyond surface-level disagreements, uncovering the underlying factors that contribute to tension.

Creating a Safe Space: Trust and Vulnerability

Effective communication requires creating a safe and nonjudgmental space where individuals can express themselves without fear of backlash or rejection. Trust is essential for this safe space to exist. When individuals feel that their thoughts and feelings are respected, they are more likely to open up and share honestly. Vulnerability in communication, where parties express their emotions and perspectives authentically, fosters empathy and lays the groundwork for conflict resolution.

Listening: The Art of Active Engagement

Listening is a cornerstone of effective communication, yet it's often overlooked or undervalued. Active listening involves not only hearing the words spoken but also understanding the emotions, concerns, and intentions behind them. When individuals truly listen to one another, they validate each other's experiences and create a sense of being heard and understood. This practice promotes connection and can de-escalate conflicts by diffusing emotional tension.

Empathy and Perspective-Taking: Bridging Divides

Empathy, the ability to understand and share the feelings of another, is a potent tool in conflict resolution. By putting oneself in another's shoes, individuals gain insight into their emotions, motivations, and needs. This insight forms the basis for compassionate communication and collaborative problem-solving. Empathy bridges divides and promotes a sense of shared understanding that is instrumental in finding resolutions that satisfy all parties.

Non-Verbal Communication: Unspoken Messages

Non-verbal cues, such as body language, facial expressions, and tone of voice, often convey more than the spoken words themselves. Paying attention to non-verbal signals is essential in effective communication, as they can reveal underlying emotions that might not be explicitly expressed. Individuals can enhance their communication skills by aligning their non-verbal cues with their verbal messages, ensuring congruence and fostering trust.

Constructive Expression: Navigating Emotional Waters

In conflicts, emotions can run high, making it challenging to express oneself constructively. Learning to express thoughts and feelings in a clear, non-confrontational manner is crucial. "I" statements, where individuals communicate their emotions without assigning blame, can prevent defensiveness and encourage a more empathetic response from the other party. Constructive expression promotes open dialogue and prevents conflicts from escalating.

The Power of Active Dialogue: Seeking Solutions

Effective communication is not just about expressing thoughts; it's about engaging in active dialogue to find solutions. Constructive conflict resolution involves collaborative problem-solving, where individuals work together to identify common interests and brainstorm win-win solutions. Through active dialogue, conflicts can be reframed from adversarial battles to joint efforts to achieve mutual understanding and resolution.

Communication as a Continuous Process

Recognizing that communication is an ongoing process is essential for effective conflict resolution. Conflict resolution is not a one-time conversation; it requires consistent and open communication to address changing circumstances, evolving emotions, and shifting perspectives. By keeping the lines of communication open and committing to ongoing dialogue, individuals ensure that conflicts are addressed comprehensively and prevent future tensions from arising.

Empowering Conflict Resolution Through Communication

Effective communication is the conduit through which conflicts are transformed into opportunities for growth and understanding. By actively listening, empathizing, and engaging in constructive expression, individuals can dismantle barriers, bridge divides, and find common ground. The role of communication in conflict resolution is a dynamic and transformative force that empowers individuals to navigate conflicts with empathy, respect, and the goal of fostering harmonious relationships.

Active Listening Techniques

Active listening is an essential skill in conflict resolution. It goes beyond merely hearing words; it involves fully engaging with the speaker, understanding their message, and empathizing with their emotions. In this chapter, we delve into the art of active listening, exploring various techniques that enhance communication, build trust, and facilitate the resolution of conflicts. By mastering these techniques, individuals can create a foundation of understanding that is vital for effective conflict resolution.

The Essence of Active Listening: Going Beyond Hearing

Active listening is a mindful and intentional process that involves focusing on the speaker, comprehending their message, and responding thoughtfully. It requires setting aside one's own thoughts and distractions to fully immerse oneself in the speaker's perspective. Through active listening, individuals demonstrate respect, empathy, and a genuine interest in understanding the speaker's point of view.

Providing Undivided Attention: Creating a Presence

To actively listen, individuals must provide their undivided attention. This means setting aside distractions such as phones, emails, and wandering thoughts. Giving the speaker one's full presence conveys that their words are valued and important. It also allows the listener to pick up on non-verbal cues and subtle emotions that contribute to a deeper understanding of the speaker's message.

Maintaining Eye Contact: A Connection of Respect

Maintaining eye contact is a non-verbal signal that communicates respect and attentiveness. It shows the speaker that their words are being heard and acknowledged. While cultural norms regarding eye contact may vary, making comfortable and appropriate eye contact helps establish a connection between the listener and speaker, fostering an environment of open communication.

Reflective Responses: Verbal Validation

Reflective responses involve paraphrasing or summarizing the speaker's words to confirm understanding. Phrases such as "What I'm hearing is..." or "If I understand correctly..." demonstrate that the listener is actively processing the information and seeking clarity. Reflective responses provide an opportunity for the speaker to confirm or correct any misinterpretations, fostering mutual understanding.

Asking Open-Ended Questions: Encouraging Elaboration

Open-ended questions encourage the speaker to elaborate on their thoughts and feelings, fostering deeper conversation. Questions like "Can you tell me more about that?" or "What was your experience like?" prompt the speaker to share additional information, allowing the listener to gain a comprehensive view of the topic. This technique not only demonstrates interest but also demonstrates a willingness to explore the issue thoroughly.

Paraphrasing Emotions: Acknowledging Feelings

Paraphrasing emotions involves recognizing and acknowledging the emotions the speaker is expressing. Phrases like "It sounds like you're feeling frustrated because..." or "I can sense that this situation has left you feeling hurt" show empathy and validation. Acknowledging emotions allows the speaker to feel understood and creates an atmosphere of emotional safety.

Avoiding Judgment: Non-Critical Listening

Active listening requires suspending judgment and refraining from offering immediate solutions or critiques. Instead of interjecting with advice or opinions, the listener focuses on absorbing the speaker's perspective. Avoiding judgment promotes an open space where the speaker can freely express themselves without fear of being evaluated or criticized.

Silence as a Tool: Allowing Processing Time

Silence is an integral part of active listening. It provides the speaker with the time and space to gather their thoughts and express themselves fully. Some individuals may need more time to articulate their feelings or gather their ideas. Embracing moments of silence shows patience and allows the speaker to lead the pace of the conversation.

Empathy and Validation: Building Emotional Bonds

Active listening inherently involves empathy and validation. By actively engaging with the speaker's emotions and experiences, the listener demonstrates that their feelings are acknowledged and respected. This builds an emotional bond between the parties, creating a foundation of trust that is essential for effective conflict resolution.

The Impact of Active Listening on Conflict Resolution

Mastering active listening techniques is a transformative skill for conflict resolution. By actively listening, individuals validate each other's perspectives, promote understanding, and create an environment conducive to finding common ground. Active listening empowers individuals to approach conflicts with empathy, respect, and a genuine desire to reach resolutions that honor the needs and emotions of all parties involved.

The Power of Non-Verbal Communication

Communication is not limited to words alone; non-verbal cues play a significant role in conveying messages, emotions, and intentions. In this chapter, we delve into the intricate world of non-verbal communication, exploring how body language, facial expressions, gestures, and tone of voice contribute to effective conflict resolution. Understanding the power of non-verbal communication equips individuals with a comprehensive toolkit for enhancing understanding, building rapport, and fostering harmonious relationships.

The Universality of Non-Verbal Cues

Non-verbal communication is universal, transcending language barriers and cultural differences. Facial expressions, for instance, convey emotions such as happiness, sadness, anger, and surprise, regardless of one's native language. Understanding these universal cues enables individuals to connect on a deeper level and bridge communication gaps that might arise from language variations.

Body Language: The Unspoken Language of the Body

Body language encompasses a range of non-verbal cues, including posture, gestures, and movement. Posture can communicate confidence, openness, or defensiveness. Gestures, such as nodding or pointing, can enhance understanding and reinforce spoken messages. Movement, whether relaxed or tense, adds layers of meaning to verbal communication. Being aware of one's own body language and attuned to others' cues enhances the effectiveness of communication.

Facial Expressions: Windows to Emotions

The face is a canvas of emotions, with facial expressions conveying a wealth of feelings. A smile can express warmth and openness, while a furrowed brow might indicate concern or confusion. Understanding facial expressions helps listeners interpret emotions and align their responses accordingly. Facial cues provide insight into the speaker's emotional state and guide active listening and empathy.

Tone of Voice: The Emotion Behind the Words

Tone of voice is a powerful aspect of non-verbal communication. The way words are spoken—whether with enthusiasm, sarcasm, anger, or kindness—can completely alter their meaning. Tone adds emotional depth to verbal messages, influencing how they are received and interpreted. Being attuned to tone allows individuals to gauge emotions accurately and respond in ways that resonate with the speaker's intentions.

Eye Contact: The Gateway to Connection

Eye contact is a crucial non-verbal cue that establishes a connection between individuals. It communicates attentiveness, interest, and respect. The duration and intensity of eye contact can vary across cultures, but the intent behind it remains consistent: to engage and connect with the speaker. Appropriate and comfortable eye contact fosters trust and promotes open communication.

Personal Space and Proximity: Respect for Boundaries

Personal space and proximity communicate comfort levels and boundaries. Individuals have varying thresholds for physical closeness, and respecting these boundaries is essential for establishing rapport. Being aware of cultural norms regarding personal space is important, as what might be considered appropriate in one culture could be invasive in another. Adhering to respectful distances fosters a sense of safety and openness.

Mirroring and Synchronization: Building Rapport

Mirroring involves subtly imitating the body language, gestures, and even speech patterns of the speaker. This non-verbal technique fosters rapport and a sense of connection, as it conveys similarity and shared understanding. Synchronization goes beyond mirroring and involves aligning one's behavior with the rhythm of the speaker's communication. These techniques create an environment of comfort and understanding.

Congruence: Aligning Verbal and Non-Verbal Messages

Congruence occurs when verbal and non-verbal messages align. When words and body language are in harmony, the listener perceives authenticity and sincerity. Incongruence—when non-verbal cues contradict spoken words—can create confusion and mistrust. Ensuring congruence between verbal and non-verbal communication enhances credibility and facilitates clearer understanding.

Cultural Considerations: Navigating Diversity

Non-verbal cues are influenced by cultural norms and can vary significantly from one culture to another. What might be interpreted as assertive in one culture could be seen as disrespectful in another. Being culturally sensitive and open to learning about non-verbal norms allows individuals to communicate effectively and respectfully across diverse backgrounds.

Enhancing Conflict Resolution through Non-Verbal Communication

Non-verbal communication adds depth and nuance to conflict resolution. Understanding and utilizing non-verbal cues enable individuals to decode emotions, validate feelings, and establish rapport. Effective non-verbal communication enhances active listening, empathy, and the overall quality of communication, making the journey toward conflict resolution smoother and more impactful.

Constructive Expression of Thoughts and Feelings

Effective communication in conflict resolution involves more than just listening; it also encompasses the skill of expressing thoughts and feelings in a way that promotes understanding and resolution. In this chapter, we explore the art of constructive expression, understanding how to communicate thoughts and emotions clearly, respectfully, and assertively. By mastering this skill, individuals can convey their perspectives while maintaining open lines of communication and fostering harmonious relationships.

The Power of Clarity: Clear Communication

Clarity is paramount when expressing thoughts and feelings in conflicts. Ambiguous or vague communication can lead to misunderstandings and further tension. Clearly articulating one's perspective, using concise language, and avoiding jargon or assumptions ensure that the message is accurately conveyed. When individuals communicate with clarity, the chances of productive dialogue and resolution increase significantly.

"I" Statements: Taking Ownership of Feelings

"I" statements, also known as "I" messages, are a powerful communication technique that focuses on expressing emotions and thoughts from a personal perspective. By starting sentences with "I feel..." or "I believe...," individuals take ownership of their emotions and avoid placing blame on others. "I" statements promote open conversation without triggering defensiveness, as they foster understanding rather than accusation.

Active and Reflective Listening in Expression

Effective expression is not a one-way street; it involves active and reflective listening. When individuals express their thoughts and feelings, they should also listen attentively to the response. This demonstrates respect for the other party's perspective and allows for a back-and-forth exchange that promotes deeper understanding. Reflecting back what was heard through paraphrasing shows that the speaker's message was truly received.

Using "I" Statements in Conflict Resolution

Applying "I" statements in conflict resolution offers a powerful approach. When discussing conflicts, individuals can use "I" statements to communicate their emotions and needs. For example, "I felt hurt when I wasn't included in the decision-making process" conveys emotions and allows for further discussion. "I" statements create a safe space for sharing feelings and promote a collaborative approach to resolution.

Assertiveness: Striking a Balance

Constructive expression requires striking a balance between assertiveness and respect. Assertiveness involves confidently expressing one's thoughts, feelings, and needs while acknowledging the perspective of others. It allows individuals to advocate for their interests without dominating the conversation or undermining others' viewpoints. Assertive communication promotes open dialogue and encourages collaboration.

Avoiding Aggressive Communication

Aggressive communication involves attacking, blaming, or belittling others. It leads to defensiveness, escalates conflicts, and erodes trust. Expressing thoughts and feelings assertively is distinct from aggression. Instead of saying, "You always do this," individuals can rephrase to focus on their emotions and needs: "I feel frustrated when this happens." This shift in communication fosters understanding and de-escalation.

Active Expression of Emotions: Emotional Honesty

Conflict resolution requires individuals to express their emotions honestly. Suppressing emotions or pretending not to be affected can hinder resolution efforts. Active expression of emotions involves acknowledging and sharing feelings while maintaining composure. For example, expressing, "I'm feeling overwhelmed and frustrated right now, but I'm committed to finding a solution" opens the door for collaboration.

Using Neutral Language: Objectivity in Expression

Neutral language is free from judgment, blame, or accusations. It focuses on the facts and one's feelings without attacking others. Instead of saying, "You're wrong," individuals can use neutral language: "I see this differently because..." Neutral language creates a less confrontational atmosphere, enabling parties to focus on issues rather than becoming entangled in personal attacks.

Reframing: Shifting Perspectives

Reframing involves presenting thoughts and feelings in a way that emphasizes common ground and shared interests. It allows individuals to shift the focus from differences to potential solutions. For instance, instead of saying, "You're not considering my point of view," individuals can reframe as: "Let's work together to find a solution that considers both perspectives." Reframing fosters collaboration and resolution.

Apologies and Forgiveness: Repairing Relationships

Constructive expression extends to apologies and forgiveness. Apologizing acknowledges any harm caused and demonstrates a commitment to repairing the relationship. Forgiveness involves letting go of resentment and moving forward. Effective apologies are sincere, take responsibility, and offer a plan for improvement. Forgiveness requires empathy and a willingness to release negative emotions to rebuild trust.

Constructive Expression as a Bridge to Resolution

Mastering the art of constructive expression is an integral step in effective conflict resolution. By using "I" statements, maintaining assertiveness and respect, and applying neutral language, individuals create a framework for open dialogue and understanding. Constructive expression empowers individuals to communicate their perspectives while fostering an atmosphere of collaboration, empathy, and the potential for harmonious resolutions.

Chapter 3: Self-Awareness in Conflict
Unveiling Your Triggers and Reactions

Self-awareness is the cornerstone of effective conflict resolution. To navigate conflicts constructively, individuals must first understand their own triggers, reactions, and emotional patterns. In this chapter, we delve into the process of unveiling your triggers and reactions, exploring how past experiences, beliefs, and emotions shape your responses in conflicts. By embracing self-awareness, individuals can gain insight into their behavior, manage their reactions, and approach conflicts with greater mindfulness and control.

The Role of Triggers in Conflict

Triggers are emotional buttons that, when pushed, evoke strong reactions. They often originate from past experiences, insecurities, and unresolved emotions. Triggers are like emotional landmines that can cause intense emotional responses in certain situations. Identifying your triggers is a crucial step toward understanding why conflicts can escalate quickly and how to manage your reactions effectively.

Exploring the Source of Triggers

Triggers often stem from significant life events, childhood experiences, or repeated patterns in relationships. For instance, if a person had experienced betrayal in the past, situations involving perceived dishonesty might trigger intense feelings of anger or defensiveness. Exploring the source of triggers helps uncover the underlying emotions and beliefs that fuel your reactions.

Recognizing Physical and Emotional Reactions

Triggers manifest in both physical and emotional reactions. Physical signs might include increased heart rate, tense muscles, or a knot in the stomach. Emotional reactions can range from anger and frustration to anxiety and sadness. Recognizing these reactions is key to understanding when you are triggered, allowing you to take steps to manage your responses.

Patterns of Behavior: Unraveling the Cycle

Triggers often lead to patterns of behavior that repeat in conflicts. For example, feeling dismissed might trigger a defensive response, leading to an escalated argument. Recognizing these patterns is crucial for breaking the cycle and responding more constructively. Self-awareness allows you to interrupt automatic reactions and choose more intentional responses.

Mindfulness: Creating Space for Awareness

Mindfulness is a practice that cultivates self-awareness by focusing on the present moment without judgment. Mindfulness enables individuals to observe their thoughts, emotions, and reactions without being consumed by them. By creating space between triggers and reactions, mindfulness provides the opportunity to choose how to respond rather than react impulsively.

Self-Reflection: Digging Deeper

Self-reflection involves introspection and examination of your thoughts, feelings, and behaviors. It's a process of digging deeper to understand why certain situations or behaviors trigger you. Journaling, meditation, and conversations with trusted individuals can facilitate self-reflection, helping you uncover patterns and gaining insight into your triggers.

Unveiling Unconscious Beliefs

Triggers often uncover unconscious beliefs and assumptions that shape your perception of conflicts. These beliefs might involve themes like worthiness, control, or acceptance. For instance, a belief that "I'm not good enough" could trigger defensive reactions when feedback is perceived as criticism. Identifying and challenging these beliefs empowers you to respond more rationally.

Emotional Intelligence: The Key to Managing Triggers

Emotional intelligence—the ability to recognize, understand, and manage your own emotions—is instrumental in managing triggers. By being attuned to your emotions, you can identify when you're becoming triggered and take steps to prevent reactive behavior. Techniques like deep breathing, grounding exercises, and taking a pause can help you manage your emotional responses.

Cultivating Emotional Regulation

Emotional regulation involves managing your emotions in ways that align with your goals and values. Instead of reacting impulsively to triggers, you can choose how to respond in a manner that promotes productive communication and resolution. Emotional regulation techniques include identifying early signs of emotional escalation, using positive self-talk, and practicing relaxation methods.

Conflict Resolution with Self-Awareness

Unveiling your triggers and reactions is a transformative step in conflict resolution. With self-awareness, you gain the ability to respond rather than react, fostering open dialogue and preventing conflicts from escalating. By understanding the emotional landscape within yourself, you pave the way for empathy, effective communication, and the potential to transform conflicts into opportunities for growth and connection.

Cultivating Emotional Intelligence

Emotional intelligence is a critical skill in conflict resolution, encompassing the ability to recognize, understand, manage, and utilize emotions effectively. In this chapter, we explore the multifaceted realm of emotional intelligence, delving into how self-awareness, self-regulation, empathy, and social skills contribute to navigating conflicts with empathy, understanding, and skillful communication. By cultivating emotional intelligence, individuals equip themselves with tools to transform conflicts into opportunities for growth, connection, and resolution.

Understanding Emotional Intelligence

Emotional intelligence (EI) is the capacity to perceive, understand, manage, and regulate emotions in oneself and others. It involves the ability to navigate emotional landscapes, respond to situations thoughtfully, and build meaningful relationships. EI comprises multiple dimensions, all of which contribute to effective conflict resolution.

Self-Awareness: The Foundation of EI

Self-awareness is the cornerstone of emotional intelligence. It involves recognizing your own emotions, understanding their origins, and acknowledging their impact on your thoughts and behaviors. In conflict resolution, self-awareness allows you to identify triggers, regulate reactions, and make conscious choices rather than succumbing to impulsive responses.

Self-Regulation: Managing Emotions Wisely

Self-regulation is the skill of managing and controlling your emotions in various situations. It involves the ability to stay composed, even in challenging circumstances, and to respond in ways that align with your values and goals. Developing self-regulation helps individuals remain calm, focused, and open-minded during conflicts, preventing emotional escalations and fostering constructive dialogue.

Empathy: Understanding Others' Emotions

Empathy is the ability to understand and share the feelings of others. It involves stepping into someone else's shoes, seeing the world from their perspective, and acknowledging their emotions without judgment. Empathy in conflict resolution helps create an atmosphere of understanding, validates others' experiences, and lays the groundwork for collaborative problem-solving.

Social Skills: Navigating Relationships Effectively

Social skills encompass the ability to build and maintain healthy relationships, communicate effectively, and resolve conflicts collaboratively. Effective communication, active listening, and assertive expression are integral components of social skills. By honing these skills, individuals can engage in open dialogue, manage differences, and find common ground, even in the midst of conflicts.

The Cycle of Emotional Intelligence

Emotional intelligence operates in a cyclical manner, with each dimension influencing the others. Self-awareness leads to better self-regulation, which in turn enhances empathy and social skills. This cycle promotes a holistic approach to conflict resolution, as each dimension strengthens the others, creating a harmonious blend of emotional intelligence competencies.

Developing Emotional Intelligence

Cultivating emotional intelligence requires intentional effort and practice. Here are some strategies to develop each dimension of EI:

- Self-Awareness: Practice self-reflection, journaling, and mindfulness to become attuned to your emotions and triggers. Regularly assess your emotional responses and their impact on your interactions.

- Self-Regulation: Develop emotional regulation techniques, such as deep breathing, visualization, and reframing negative thoughts. Engage in activities like meditation or yoga to promote emotional balance.

- Empathy: Practice active listening, seeking to understand the emotions and perspectives of others. Engage in perspective-taking exercises, imagining scenarios from different viewpoints to broaden your empathy.

- Social Skills: Hone your communication skills by practicing active listening, effective expression, and conflict resolution techniques. Seek opportunities to engage in group discussions, teamwork, and collaborative problem-solving.

Emotional Intelligence and Conflict Resolution

Emotional intelligence significantly influences the quality of conflict resolution. By cultivating emotional intelligence, individuals gain the ability to:

- Recognize their own emotions and triggers, preventing reactive behavior.

- Regulate their emotional responses, maintaining composure during conflicts.

- Empathize with others, fostering understanding and connection.

- Utilize social skills to engage in open dialogue and collaborative problem-solving.

Emotional Intelligence in Action

Imagine two individuals engaged in a conflict. One with high emotional intelligence approaches the situation with self-awareness, acknowledges their emotions, and regulates their reactions. They listen empathetically, express their thoughts assertively, and navigate the conflict with emotional balance. The other person, lacking emotional intelligence, reacts impulsively, escalates tensions, and struggles to communicate effectively.

The Benefits of Developing EI

Cultivating emotional intelligence brings numerous benefits to conflict resolution:

- Reduced emotional escalations and misunderstandings.
- Enhanced empathy and understanding.
- Improved communication and collaboration.
- Greater self-control and emotional balance.
- Strengthened relationships and a foundation for harmonious interactions.

Emotional Intelligence: A Lifelong Journey

Developing emotional intelligence is a lifelong journey. It requires consistent self-reflection, practice, and a willingness to learn from each conflict encountered. By cultivating emotional intelligence, individuals empower themselves to navigate conflicts with grace, empathy, and the intention of transforming them into opportunities for personal growth and strengthened relationships.

The Art of Self-Reflection

Self-reflection is a powerful practice that deepens self-awareness, enhances emotional intelligence, and enriches conflict resolution skills. In this chapter, we delve into the art of self-reflection, exploring how introspection, contemplation, and self-examination contribute to understanding triggers, emotions, and reactions. By mastering the art of self-reflection, individuals can approach conflicts with greater clarity, empathy, and the capacity for transformative resolutions.

Understanding Self-Reflection

Self-reflection involves looking inward to examine your thoughts, emotions, behaviors, and experiences. It's a process of contemplation and introspection that allows you to gain insights into your inner world. By taking the time to reflect, you can uncover patterns, understand your motivations, and make more intentional choices in conflicts.

The Benefits of Self-Reflection

Self-reflection offers a multitude of benefits, especially in conflict resolution:

- Insight into Triggers: Self-reflection helps you identify your triggers—those emotional hot buttons that can ignite conflicts. Recognizing triggers empowers you to manage them more effectively.

- Awareness of Emotions: By reflecting on your emotional responses, you can understand the range of emotions that arise during conflicts and the impact they have on your communication.

- Clarification of Intentions: Self-reflection helps you clarify your intentions and motivations in conflicts. Are you seeking resolution, validation, or control? Understanding your intentions guides your approach.

- Insight into Reactions: Examining your reactions to conflicts reveals patterns of behavior. Do you tend to become defensive, avoidant, or confrontational? This awareness allows you to choose more constructive responses.

- Empathy Development: Self-reflection fosters empathy by encouraging you to consider others' perspectives, feelings, and needs. This empathetic understanding is essential for effective conflict resolution.

- Enhanced Self-Control: Reflecting on past conflicts helps you recognize moments when you could have responded differently. This awareness cultivates self-control and equips you to make more conscious choices.

Practicing Self-Reflection

Here are steps to embrace the art of self-reflection:

1. Create Space: Find a quiet, comfortable space where you can engage in self-reflection without distractions. This

might involve setting aside time each day or dedicating moments after conflicts.

2. Journaling: Writing is a powerful tool for self-reflection. In a journal, record your thoughts, feelings, and observations about conflicts. As you write, you might uncover insights and patterns.

3. Guiding Questions: Use guiding questions to steer your reflection. Questions like "What triggered my reaction?" or "How did I contribute to this conflict?" prompt deep contemplation.

4. Mindful Awareness: Practice mindfulness as you reflect. Pay attention to your thoughts, emotions, and bodily sensations without judgment. Mindfulness enhances self-awareness.

5. Contemplation: Take time to contemplate your experiences. Consider your role, your emotional responses, and the dynamics of the conflict. Contemplation allows for a deeper understanding.

6. Feedback Incorporation: Reflect on feedback received from others during conflicts. Assess whether the feedback resonates with your self-perception and explore areas for growth.

7. Reframing Perspectives: During self-reflection, challenge your assumptions and beliefs. Consider alternative viewpoints and how they might impact your responses.

The Role of Self-Compassion

Self-reflection should be approached with self-compassion—a kind and nonjudgmental attitude toward yourself. Recognize that conflicts are opportunities for growth, and mistakes are part of the learning process. Instead of criticizing yourself, acknowledge areas for improvement and celebrate your progress.

Building a Habit of Self-Reflection

Consistency is key to making self-reflection a habit:

- Set Aside Time: Allocate a specific time for self-reflection. Regularity enhances the effectiveness of this practice.

- Incorporate Daily Reflection: Reflect on your interactions and reactions each day. Consider what went well and where you could have responded differently.

- Learning from Conflicts: After resolving conflicts, take time to reflect on the experience. What did you learn? How can you apply this knowledge in the future?

Integration of Self-Reflection in Conflict Resolution

Imagine a scenario where a conflict arises. Without self-reflection, you might react based on instinct or habit.

With self-reflection, you pause, examine your emotions, triggers, and intentions. You consider the other party's perspective, assess your role, and choose a response aligned with your values and goals. Self-reflection transforms conflicts from reactive battlegrounds to opportunities for conscious growth and resolution.

The Journey of Self-Reflection

Self-reflection is a journey that requires patience and ongoing commitment. Through introspection and contemplation, you unearth layers of self-awareness that enhance your conflict resolution abilities. As you cultivate the art of self-reflection, conflicts become invitations to understand yourself and others more deeply, fostering empathy, clarity, and a pathway to transformative resolutions.

Mindfulness Practices for Conflict Resolution

Mindfulness is a powerful practice that enhances self-awareness, emotional intelligence, and conflict resolution skills. In this chapter, we delve into the realm of mindfulness, exploring how mindfulness practices can be applied to conflicts to promote clarity, empathy, and effective communication. By embracing mindfulness, individuals can navigate conflicts with presence, compassion, and the ability to transform challenges into opportunities for growth and connection.

Understanding Mindfulness

Mindfulness involves being fully present in the current moment without judgment. It's the practice of observing your thoughts, emotions, and physical sensations without being consumed by them. By cultivating mindfulness, you develop the capacity to respond intentionally rather than reacting impulsively to conflicts.

The Role of Mindfulness in Conflict Resolution

Mindfulness plays a pivotal role in conflict resolution by:

- Enhancing Self-Awareness: Mindfulness enables you to recognize your emotions, triggers, and thought patterns during conflicts. This awareness empowers you to choose responses that align with your intentions.

- Promoting Empathy: Mindfulness fosters empathy by encouraging you to fully engage with the perspectives and emotions of others. This deep understanding forms the basis for compassionate communication.

- Reducing Reactivity: Mindfulness helps you regulate your emotional responses. By observing your reactions without judgment, you create space to choose how you'll respond, rather than reacting impulsively.

- Improving Communication: Mindfulness encourages active listening and presence during conversations. This attentive communication fosters open dialogue and prevents misunderstandings.

- Creating Emotional Balance: Mindfulness equips you to manage intense emotions during conflicts. By acknowledging emotions without being consumed by them, you can approach conflicts with emotional balance.

Mindfulness Practices for Conflict Resolution

Here are mindfulness practices that can be integrated into conflict resolution:

1. Mindful Breathing: Focus on your breath to anchor yourself in the present moment. During conflicts, take deep, intentional breaths to regulate your emotions and remain centered.

2. Body Scan: Practice body scan meditation to become aware of physical sensations. This practice helps you notice tension and stress in your body during conflicts, allowing you to release them.

3. Observing Thoughts: Notice your thoughts without judgment. Instead of getting caught up in negative self-talk or assumptions, observe your thoughts as passing clouds.

4. Mindful Listening: Practice active listening during conflicts. Fully engage with the speaker's words, maintaining eye contact and avoiding distractions. This focused attention enhances understanding.

5. Pausing: When conflicts escalate, take a mindful pause. Step away from the situation, take a few deep breaths, and observe your emotions before re-engaging in a more composed manner.

6. Labeling Emotions: During conflicts, label your emotions. By naming them—such as "frustration" or "anxiety"—you create distance between yourself and the emotions, reducing their intensity.

7. Non-Judgmental Observation: Observe your thoughts, emotions, and reactions without labeling them as good or bad. This non-judgmental approach promotes self-compassion.

Applying Mindfulness in Conflict Scenarios

Imagine you're in a conflict with a colleague. Without mindfulness, you might react defensively or emotionally. With mindfulness, you pause, observe your emotions and thoughts, and choose to respond empathetically. You actively listen to their perspective, regulate your emotions, and communicate your own thoughts more effectively. Mindfulness transforms the conflict into an opportunity for meaningful dialogue and resolution.

Mindfulness: A Way of Being

Mindfulness is not just a practice; it's a way of being. By integrating mindfulness into your daily life, conflicts become chances to embody presence, empathy, and self-awareness. As you embrace mindfulness, you bring a sense of calm and clarity to conflicts, fostering an atmosphere of respect and collaboration.

Building a Mindfulness Habit

To make mindfulness a habit:

- Consistent Practice: Dedicate time each day to mindfulness exercises. Gradually, mindfulness will become a natural part of your interactions.

- Incorporate Mindfulness in Routine: Infuse mindfulness into daily activities. Practice mindful eating, walking, or even conversations with loved ones.

- Gentle Persistence: Be patient with yourself. Mindfulness is a skill that develops over time. Approach it with curiosity and an open heart.

Transforming Conflicts through Mindfulness

Mindfulness empowers you to transform conflicts from confrontations to opportunities for growth and connection. By being present, empathetic, and aware of your reactions, you navigate conflicts with intention and compassion. Mindfulness transforms conflicts into moments of self-discovery, learning, and building relationships based on understanding and mutual respect.

Chapter 4: Empathy and Perspective-Taking

The Importance of Empathy in Resolving Conflicts

Empathy is a cornerstone of effective conflict resolution, enabling individuals to connect on a deep level, understand diverse perspectives, and foster mutual understanding. In this chapter, we explore the profound significance of empathy in resolving conflicts, delving into its components, benefits, and practical applications. By embracing empathy, individuals can transform conflicts into opportunities for connection, growth, and collaborative solutions.

Understanding Empathy

Empathy is the ability to understand and share the emotions, perspectives, and experiences of others. It involves stepping into someone else's shoes and imagining the world from their point of view. Empathy doesn't necessarily mean agreeing with another's perspective, but it does mean validating their emotions and demonstrating a willingness to understand.

The Core Components of Empathy

Empathy is multifaceted and can be divided into three core components:

1. Cognitive Empathy: This involves understanding another person's perspective, thoughts, and feelings. It's the capacity to grasp where they're coming from intellectually.

2. Emotional Empathy: Emotional empathy involves feeling the emotions of others as if they were your own. It allows you to share in someone's emotional experience and offer genuine support.

3. Empathetic Concern: Also known as compassionate empathy, this component involves not only understanding and feeling another's emotions but also being moved to take action to alleviate their distress.

Empathy in Conflict Resolution

Empathy is indispensable in resolving conflicts for several reasons:

1. Building Trust: Empathy builds trust by showing that you genuinely care about another's feelings and experiences. Trust is essential for open communication and collaboration.

2. Reducing Defensiveness: When someone feels understood and validated, they're less likely to become defensive. Empathy creates an environment where individuals are more willing to listen and engage constructively.

3. Enhancing Communication: Empathy promotes active listening and allows you to ask questions that deepen your understanding of others' perspectives. This clear communication is crucial for conflict resolution.

4. Promoting Collaboration: Empathy opens the door to collaborative problem-solving. When all parties feel heard and valued, they're more likely to work together to find win-win solutions.

5. Humanizing Interactions: Conflict often dehumanizes individuals, reducing them to opposing viewpoints. Empathy restores the human element, fostering respect and compassion.

Challenges and Barriers to Empathy

While empathy is powerful, it can be hindered by various challenges:

1. Bias and Prejudice: Our biases and prejudices can affect our ability to empathize with certain individuals or groups.

2. Emotional Overload: Feeling others' emotions intensely can lead to emotional fatigue or burnout, making it challenging to maintain empathy consistently.

3. Misunderstandings: Misinterpreting another person's emotions or perspective can hinder accurate empathy.

4. Conflict Dynamics: In the midst of conflicts, emotions can run high, making it difficult to remain empathetic and composed.

Cultivating Empathy

Cultivating empathy is a lifelong journey that requires deliberate effort:

1. Active Listening: Engage in active listening, focusing on understanding the speaker rather than formulating your response.

2. Perspective-Taking: Imagine yourself in the other person's situation. How would you feel? What thoughts might you have?

3. Questioning: Ask open-ended questions to encourage the other party to share their thoughts and emotions.

4. Reflective Practice: Regularly reflect on your interactions to assess how empathetic you were and how you can improve.

5. Mindfulness: Being present in the moment enhances your capacity for empathy by allowing you to fully engage with the other person.

Empathy in Practice

Imagine a conflict between colleagues over project priorities. Without empathy, the conflict might escalate, with both parties entrenched in their positions. With empathy, each person takes the time to listen, understand, and validate the other's concerns. As a result, they collaboratively find a solution that benefits both individuals and the organization.

Empathy as a Transformative Force

Empathy has the power to transform conflicts from adversarial battles to opportunities for understanding and connection. By seeing conflicts through the lens of empathy, individuals transcend their own viewpoints and embrace the rich tapestry of human experiences. Empathy bridges gaps, nurtures trust, and paves the way for meaningful resolutions that honor the diversity of perspectives and emotions involved.

Practicing Perspective-Taking

Perspective-taking is a fundamental skill in conflict resolution, allowing individuals to transcend their own viewpoints and understand the world through the eyes of others. In this chapter, we explore the art of perspective-taking, its significance in conflicts, and practical strategies to enhance this skill. By mastering perspective-taking, individuals can build bridges of understanding, empathy, and collaboration, fostering resolutions that honor diverse perspectives.

Understanding Perspective-Taking

Perspective-taking involves stepping into another person's shoes and viewing a situation from their vantage point. It requires setting aside your own biases and assumptions to genuinely understand another's thoughts, feelings, and motivations. Perspective-taking doesn't require agreement; it's about acknowledging and respecting the validity of someone else's experience.

The Role of Perspective-Taking in Conflict Resolution

Perspective-taking is invaluable in resolving conflicts for several reasons:

1. Broadening Understanding: By considering multiple viewpoints, you gain a more comprehensive understanding of the conflict's nuances and complexities.

2. Reducing Misunderstandings: Misunderstandings often arise from differing perspectives. Perspective-taking helps clarify intentions and diminish misinterpretations.

3. Promoting Empathy: Perspective-taking fosters empathy by allowing you to emotionally connect with another's experiences and emotions.

4. Humanizing Interactions: Conflict can dehumanize individuals, reducing them to opposing positions. Perspective-taking restores humanity to interactions.

5. Opening Communication: When you show that you're willing to understand someone else's perspective, they're more likely to reciprocate, creating an environment for productive dialogue.

Practical Strategies for Perspective-Taking

1. Listen Actively: During conflicts, practice active listening. Focus on the speaker's words without forming judgments or preparing counterarguments.

2. Suspend Judgment: Set aside your biases and preconceived notions. Approach the situation with an open mind.

3. Ask Questions: Engage in curious inquiry. Ask questions that encourage the other party to share their thoughts, emotions, and reasoning.

4. Imagine Their Position: Visualize the conflict from the other person's point of view. How might their experiences and emotions differ from yours?

5. Consider Their Background: Take into account the person's background, experiences, and values. These factors shape their perspective.

6. Empathize with Emotions: Try to understand the emotions underlying their perspective. What might they be feeling, and why?

Challenges and Barriers to Perspective-Taking

Perspective-taking can be challenging due to various factors:

1. Confirmation Bias: Our tendency to seek information that confirms our existing beliefs can hinder genuine perspective-taking.

2. Emotional Attachment: Strong emotions can cloud our ability to consider others' perspectives objectively.

3. Time and Patience: Perspective-taking requires time and patience to truly understand another's viewpoint.

Cultivating Perspective-Taking

Cultivating perspective-taking involves deliberate practice and self-awareness:

1. Expand Your Horizons: Seek out diverse viewpoints through conversations, reading, and engaging with individuals from different backgrounds.

2. Reflect on Your Biases: Regularly reflect on your biases and how they might influence your perceptions of others.

3. Practice Mindfulness: Mindfulness enhances your ability to be present and fully engaged in understanding others' perspectives.

4. Feedback Incorporation: After conflicts, seek feedback on your perspective-taking. Did you accurately understand the other person's viewpoint?

5. Embrace Humility: Acknowledge that your perspective isn't the only valid one. Embrace humility as you strive to understand others.

The Transformative Power of Perspective-Taking

Imagine a family conflict involving generational differences. Without perspective-taking, each generation might dismiss the other's opinions. With perspective-taking, family members listen to each other's experiences and viewpoints. They learn how cultural contexts shaped differing opinions and bridge the gap through understanding. Perspective-taking transforms the conflict into an opportunity for intergenerational connection and learning.

A Bridge to Resolutions

Perspective-taking is a bridge between conflicting viewpoints, promoting empathy, understanding, and collaboration. By transcending your own perspective, you honor the diversity of human experiences and create a foundation for resolutions that respect the richness of multiple viewpoints. Perspective-taking fosters unity amidst diversity, turning conflicts into stepping stones toward deeper connections and shared solutions.

Building Bridges through Empathetic Communication

Empathetic communication is a dynamic tool that bridges gaps, fosters understanding, and facilitates collaborative conflict resolution. In this chapter, we delve into the art of empathetic communication, its pivotal role in resolving conflicts, and practical strategies for cultivating this essential skill. By mastering empathetic communication, individuals can turn conflicts into transformative dialogues that lead to shared understanding and effective solutions.

Understanding Empathetic Communication

Empathetic communication goes beyond words; it involves listening deeply, understanding emotions, and responding with compassion. It's about creating a safe space for individuals to express themselves openly, without fear of judgment. Empathetic communication acknowledges the human dimension of conflicts and nurtures relationships amidst disagreement.

The Importance of Empathetic Communication in Conflict Resolution

Empathetic communication is a cornerstone of conflict resolution due to its many benefits:

1. Fostering Trust: When people feel heard and understood, trust flourishes. Trust is essential for open dialogue and collaborative problem-solving.

2. Reducing Hostility: Empathetic communication softens the edges of conflict, reducing defensiveness and creating a less adversarial atmosphere.

3. Enhancing Understanding: By actively listening and understanding emotions, you gain insights into the underlying issues of conflicts.

4. Promoting Emotional Connection: Empathetic communication validates emotions, creating an emotional connection between parties.

5. Encouraging Openness: When individuals sense empathy, they're more likely to share their thoughts and feelings, creating a conducive environment for resolution.

Practical Strategies for Empathetic Communication

1. Active Listening: Devote your full attention to the speaker. Maintain eye contact, avoid distractions, and show through body language that you're engaged.

2. Reflective Listening: Paraphrase what you've heard to ensure you've understood correctly. This shows the speaker that you're actively trying to comprehend their perspective.

3. Ask Open-Ended Questions: Questions that require more than a yes or no answer encourage the speaker to share their thoughts and emotions.

4. Validate Emotions: Acknowledge the speaker's emotions without judgment. Phrases like "I can understand why you'd feel that way" show empathy.

5. Avoid Interrupting: Allow the speaker to finish before responding. Interrupting can impede their flow and hinder effective communication.

6. Express Understanding: Show that you're trying to understand by saying phrases like "I see where you're coming from" or "That makes sense."

Challenges and Barriers to Empathetic Communication

Empathetic communication can face obstacles:

1. Emotional Distance: Emotions can make it challenging to remain empathetic and composed during conflicts.

2. Assumption and Judgment: Assuming you understand someone's perspective without truly listening can hinder empathy.

3. Misinterpretation: Misinterpreting emotions or motives can lead to inaccurate empathetic responses.

Cultivating Empathetic Communication

Cultivating empathetic communication is a gradual process:

1. Self-Awareness: Understand your own emotional triggers and biases that might hinder empathetic communication.

2. Mindful Presence: Be present in conversations, fully engaging with the speaker rather than planning your response.

3. Empathy Building: Practice perspective-taking to enhance your ability to understand others' emotions and viewpoints.

4. Feedback Integration: Seek feedback from trusted individuals about your empathetic communication. What areas can you improve?

Empathetic Communication in Action

Imagine a workplace conflict between two team members. Without empathetic communication, accusations and defensiveness might escalate the conflict. With empathetic communication, one team member listens actively, validates the other's frustrations, and acknowledges their perspective. This opens the door for a productive conversation that addresses concerns and identifies collaborative solutions.

Empathy's Ripple Effect

Empathetic communication is like a ripple in a pond; it starts small but expands to touch everything it encounters. By fostering understanding, compassion, and connection, empathetic communication creates a ripple effect that transforms individual conflicts into opportunities for growth, mutual respect, and shared resolutions. Through empathetic communication, bridges are built that span divides and lead to harmonious resolutions.

Empathy's Role in Reducing Misunderstandings

Empathy is a powerful antidote to misunderstandings, offering a lens through which conflicts can be reframed and resolved. In this chapter, we explore the profound role of empathy in mitigating misunderstandings during conflicts. Through examining its impact, benefits, and practical applications, we reveal how empathy can transform misunderstandings into opportunities for connection and clarity, fostering effective conflict resolution.

The Complex Nature of Misunderstandings

Misunderstandings often arise due to differences in communication styles, cultural backgrounds, emotional interpretations, or assumptions. These misinterpretations can fuel conflicts, escalate emotions, and hinder productive dialogue.

The Power of Empathy in Reducing Misunderstandings

Empathy plays a pivotal role in untangling misunderstandings for several reasons:

1. Perspective Integration: Empathy enables individuals to view a situation from multiple angles, unveiling different viewpoints and revealing the root causes of misunderstandings.

2. Emotional Resonance: Empathy allows you to grasp the emotions underlying someone's perspective. This understanding clarifies emotional nuances that might contribute to misunderstandings.

3. Active Listening: Empathetic listening promotes accurate comprehension, reducing the chances of misinterpreting information or intentions.

4. Open Dialogue: Empathy fosters an environment where parties feel comfortable sharing their perspectives and clarifying potential misunderstandings.

5. Shared Understanding: Through empathy, individuals can collectively arrive at a shared understanding of the situation, dispelling confusion.

Benefits of Empathy in Misunderstanding Resolution

Empathy offers a host of benefits when applied to resolving misunderstandings:

1. De-escalation: Empathetic communication diffuses tension and hostility, making it easier to address misunderstandings calmly.

2. Enhanced Communication: Empathy encourages open and honest conversations, allowing parties to clarify intentions, emotions, and perspectives.

3. Emotional Validation: By validating emotions, empathy acknowledges that feelings are valid even if they stem from misunderstandings.

4. Mutual Respect: Empathy cultivates respect for each individual's unique perspective, fostering an atmosphere of collaboration.

5. Conflict Prevention: Empathy helps prevent future misunderstandings by fostering open communication and promoting the habit of clarifying intentions.

Practical Strategies for Using Empathy to Reduce Misunderstandings

1. Inquire with Curiosity: Instead of assuming, ask open-ended questions to understand the other person's point of view and emotions.

2. Paraphrase and Reflect: Paraphrase what you've heard to ensure accurate comprehension. Reflect back the emotions you've sensed.

3. Acknowledge Emotions: Validate the emotions expressed by the other person, even if they stem from misunderstandings.

4. Clarify Intentions: Share your own perspective and clarify your intentions to ensure they align with what you meant.

5. Use "I" Statements: Express how you're feeling and how you've interpreted the situation. This opens the door for clarification.

Challenges and Barriers to Using Empathy for Misunderstanding Resolution

Certain challenges can hinder empathy's effectiveness in resolving misunderstandings:

1. Emotional Reactivity: Strong emotions can cloud your capacity to approach misunderstandings empathetically.

2. Bias and Prejudice: Unconscious biases can affect your ability to empathize with individuals from different backgrounds.

3. Assumptions: Assuming you know another person's perspective without seeking clarification can undermine empathy.

Cultivating Empathy for Misunderstanding Resolution

Cultivating empathy requires consistent effort and self-awareness:

1. Self-Reflection: Regularly reflect on your own biases, triggers, and assumptions that might hinder empathetic understanding.

2. Educate Yourself: Learn about different communication styles, cultural norms, and emotional expressions to broaden your perspective.

3. Practice Perspective-Taking: Engage in exercises that help you see situations from others' viewpoints.

4. Open-Mindedness: Approach misunderstandings with an open mind, eager to uncover the truth rather than confirm preconceived notions.

Empathy's Impact in Action

Imagine a miscommunication between friends that escalates into a disagreement. Without empathy, blame and frustration might persist. With empathy, each friend listens intently to the other's viewpoint, acknowledging their emotions and clarifying intentions. This empathy-driven exchange unravels the misunderstanding, fostering understanding, and nurturing the friendship.

Transforming Misunderstandings through Empathy

Empathy is the bridge that connects differing perspectives, illuminating the heart of misunderstandings. By embracing empathy, individuals can unravel the knots of confusion, clarify intentions, and transform conflicts into collaborative dialogues. Empathy's role in reducing misunderstandings empowers individuals to navigate conflicts with compassion, transforming the landscape of misunderstandings into fertile ground for growth, connection, and effective resolution.

Chapter 5: De-Escalation Techniques

Understanding Escalation and Its Dangers

Escalation in conflicts is a phenomenon that can quickly turn minor disagreements into heated disputes. In this chapter, we delve into the intricacies of escalation, its various stages, and the potential dangers it poses. By comprehending the dynamics of escalation, individuals can proactively address conflicts, implement de-escalation strategies, and create an environment conducive to constructive resolution.

The Nature of Escalation

Escalation refers to the process by which conflicts intensify and grow more contentious over time. It often occurs due to unaddressed issues, heightened emotions, and ineffective communication. Escalation can transform manageable disagreements into hostile confrontations, negatively impacting relationships and impeding productive conflict resolution.

The Stages of Escalation

Escalation follows a pattern that unfolds through distinct stages:

1. Latent Conflict: Underlying issues exist but are not yet openly acknowledged. Tensions may simmer beneath the surface.

2. Perceived Conflict: Disagreements become more apparent, and individuals start to view each other as opponents.

3. Felt Conflict: Emotions intensify, and parties become emotionally invested in the conflict. Communication becomes more hostile.

4. Manifest Conflict: The conflict becomes visible to others. Communication breaks down further, and positions become more entrenched.

5. Conflict Aftermath: After the conflict, emotions may linger, and resentment can grow. Future interactions might be strained.

The Dangers of Escalation

Escalation carries significant dangers that can harm individuals and relationships:

1. Loss of Rationality: As emotions escalate, rational thinking and effective communication become increasingly difficult.

2. Impaired Judgment: People may make hasty decisions driven by strong emotions rather than careful consideration.

3. Damaged Relationships: Escalation strains relationships, eroding trust and mutual respect.

4. Missed Opportunities: As conflicts escalate, individuals may focus on "winning" rather than finding collaborative solutions.

5. Negative Psychological Impact: The stress of escalated conflicts can take a toll on mental and emotional well-being.

Identifying Early Warning Signs

Recognizing the early signs of escalation is crucial for preventing its progression:

1. Increased Emotionality: Heightened emotions, such as anger or frustration, may become more prevalent.

2. Repetitive Patterns: The same issues resurface without being resolved, indicating an escalating cycle.

3. Verbal Aggression: Communication becomes more confrontational and aggressive.

4. Physical Cues: Body language, such as clenched fists or raised voices, may indicate escalating emotions.

5. Avoidance: Individuals might avoid interactions or discussions due to fear of conflict.

The Need for De-Escalation

De-escalation techniques are essential for breaking the cycle of escalation, fostering effective communication, and preventing conflicts from spiraling out of control.

Creating an Environment for De-Escalation

To effectively manage escalation, it's essential to create an environment conducive to de-escalation:

1. Safety: Ensure both physical and emotional safety for all parties involved.
2. Respectful Communication: Promote respectful and open communication where individuals feel heard and understood.
3. Neutral Ground: Choose a neutral and private space for discussions to minimize distractions and defensiveness.
4. Empathy: Encourage individuals to consider each other's feelings and perspectives to reduce hostility.
5. Ground Rules: Establish ground rules for communication that promote civility and effective dialogue.

The Role of Self-Awareness

Self-awareness is a crucial element in de-escalation:

1. Recognize Triggers: Understand your own triggers and emotional reactions to prevent personal escalation.
2. Practice Emotional Regulation: Develop strategies to manage strong emotions during conflicts.
3. Pause and Reflect: When conflicts arise, take a moment to pause, reflect, and consider potential consequences.

De-Escalation Techniques in Action

Imagine a workplace conflict between colleagues regarding project responsibilities. Without de-escalation, the conflict might escalate into a shouting match. By implementing de-escalation techniques, such as choosing a neutral space, using "I" statements, and focusing on mutual goals, the colleagues engage in a constructive conversation. The conflict de-escalates, emotions subside, and they collaboratively find a solution.

Harnessing De-Escalation for Effective Resolution

Understanding the stages and dangers of escalation empowers individuals to intervene proactively, prevent conflicts from spiraling, and promote healthy communication. By creating a safe space for de-escalation, individuals can harness this vital tool to transform conflicts into opportunities for understanding, compromise, and collaborative resolution. Through de-escalation, conflicts are navigated with poise, turning potential confrontations into pathways to effective and sustainable solutions.

Strategies for Preventing Conflict Escalation

Conflict escalation can have detrimental effects on relationships and outcomes. In this chapter, we explore proactive strategies for preventing conflicts from spiraling into higher levels of intensity. By identifying triggers, fostering open communication, and implementing preventive measures, individuals can effectively navigate conflicts and create an environment conducive to constructive resolution.

Understanding Conflict Escalation

Conflict escalation involves the gradual intensification of conflicts, often driven by unaddressed issues, heightened emotions, and ineffective communication. Preventing escalation requires recognizing its early signs and employing proactive measures to halt its progression.

The Significance of Preventing Escalation

Preventing conflict escalation is crucial for several reasons:

1. Preserving Relationships: Escalation strains relationships and can lead to irreparable damage if left unchecked.

2. Enhancing Productivity: Escalated conflicts divert time and energy away from productive activities.

3. Maintaining Mental Health: High-stress conflict environments can negatively impact mental and emotional well-being.

4. Promoting Effective Communication: Preventing escalation fosters an environment where parties can communicate openly and collaboratively.

Strategies for Preventing Conflict Escalation

1. Early Intervention: Address conflicts as soon as they arise to prevent them from festering and intensifying.

2. Open Communication: Foster an environment where individuals feel comfortable sharing their concerns, preventing misunderstandings.

3. Active Listening: Pay close attention to verbal and nonverbal cues to ensure accurate understanding and demonstrate empathy.

4. Empathetic Approach: Show understanding and compassion to validate emotions and de-escalate confrontational dynamics.

5. Clarify Intentions: Misunderstandings often stem from misinterpretations. Clarify intentions to prevent miscommunications.

6. Set Clear Boundaries: Establish ground rules for communication and behavior to maintain respectful interactions.

7. Focus on Solutions: Shift the focus from assigning blame to collaboratively finding solutions.

8. Acknowledge Emotions: Validate emotions to create an atmosphere where parties feel heard and valued.

Identifying Triggers and Underlying Issues

Recognizing triggers that contribute to conflict escalation is essential:

1. Personal Triggers: Identify individual triggers, such as specific behaviors or comments, that lead to emotional reactions.

2. Underlying Issues: Dig deeper to uncover the root causes of conflicts, addressing fundamental concerns.

3. Past Experiences: Understand how past experiences and unresolved conflicts might influence current reactions.

Fostering Emotional Intelligence

Emotional intelligence plays a pivotal role in preventing escalation:

1. Self-Awareness: Recognize your own emotions and triggers to manage them effectively.

2. Empathy: Understand others' perspectives and emotions to prevent misunderstandings.

3. Emotion Regulation: Develop strategies to manage emotions during conflicts, preventing emotional escalation.

Mindful Communication for Prevention

Mindful communication is a powerful preventive tool:

1. Pause and Reflect: When conflicts arise, take a moment to pause and reflect before responding impulsively.

2. Non-Defensive Communication: Respond without defensiveness, focusing on understanding rather than proving a point.

3. Use "I" Statements: Express your feelings and thoughts using "I" statements to avoid blame and accusation.

Conflict Resolution Training

Providing conflict resolution training to individuals and teams can equip them with the skills to prevent escalation:

1. Active Listening Workshops: Teach active listening techniques to enhance understanding and empathy.

2. Emotional Intelligence Training: Develop emotional intelligence skills to navigate conflicts with grace and empathy.

3. Communication Strategies: Educate individuals about effective communication strategies that prevent misunderstandings.

Preventing Escalation in Action

Imagine a family conflict arising from differing opinions on a holiday destination. Without prevention, the disagreement might escalate into a full-blown argument. By implementing prevention strategies—such as clarifying intentions, validating emotions, and actively listening—the family engages in a productive discussion. The conflict remains at a manageable level, and they collaboratively decide on a destination.

Harnessing Prevention for Lasting Resolutions

Understanding the triggers of escalation and implementing preventive strategies empowers individuals to navigate conflicts effectively. By fostering open communication, promoting empathy, and addressing underlying concerns, conflicts can be defused before they intensify. Through proactive prevention, conflicts are transformed into opportunities for growth, connection, and collaborative resolution, creating an environment where conflicts are addressed constructively and relationships are preserved.

Diffusing Tensions through Calmness and Understanding

De-escalating tensions requires a composed approach that prioritizes understanding and emotional regulation. In this chapter, we delve into the art of diffusing tensions by fostering calmness and empathy. By mastering techniques that promote emotional balance and empathetic communication, individuals can navigate conflicts with grace, prevent escalation, and forge a path towards resolution and reconciliation.

The Role of Calmness in Conflict Resolution

Calmness is a potent antidote to escalating tensions. It allows individuals to approach conflicts with clarity, empathy, and rationality. When emotions run high, responding with calmness prevents conflicts from spiraling into hostility and opens space for productive dialogue.

Cultivating Calmness in Conflicts

Cultivating calmness is a multifaceted process that involves:

1. Emotion Regulation: Develop strategies to manage strong emotions, such as deep breathing, mindfulness, and positive self-talk.

2. Pause and Reflect: Before responding, take a moment to pause and reflect on your emotions, intentions, and potential outcomes.

3. Physical Relaxation: Practice relaxation techniques, like progressive muscle relaxation, to alleviate physical tension.

4. Mindful Awareness: Cultivate mindfulness to stay present in the moment, reducing reactivity and fostering composure.

Empathy's Role in Diffusing Tensions

Empathy is a bridge that connects conflicting parties through shared understanding. Its role in diffusing tensions is profound:

1. Emotional Validation: Empathy acknowledges emotions, making individuals feel heard and understood.

2. Neutralizing Defensiveness: When individuals sense empathy, defensiveness subsides, creating a conducive environment for dialogue.

3. Building Bridges: Empathy builds connections between conflicting parties, paving the way for cooperative conflict resolution.

4. Fostering Collaboration: Empathy encourages collaboration by emphasizing shared goals and mutual understanding.

Practical Strategies for Diffusing Tensions

1. Stay Calm: Respond to conflicts with a composed demeanor, modeling the behavior you want to encourage.

2. Active Listening: Listen attentively to the other party's perspective, demonstrating your willingness to understand.

3. Validate Emotions: Acknowledge the emotions expressed by the other person without judgment.

4. Use "I" Statements: Express your feelings and thoughts using "I" statements to avoid sounding accusatory.

5. Seek Common Ground: Identify shared goals or interests to create a foundation for cooperation.

6. Take Breaks: If tensions escalate, suggest taking a short break to cool down before resuming the discussion.

Diffusing Tensions in Action

Imagine a disagreement between colleagues about project responsibilities that has escalated into a heated argument. Without intervention, the argument might disrupt teamwork and morale. By diffusing tensions through calmness and understanding, one colleague listens actively and validates the other's concerns. They acknowledge shared goals and explore collaborative solutions. The tension subsides, and the colleagues work together more harmoniously.

The Ripple Effect of Calmness and Understanding

Calmness and understanding have a ripple effect that extends beyond the immediate conflict:

1. Positive Atmosphere: Diffusing tensions creates a positive atmosphere where individuals feel valued and respected.

2. Enhanced Relationships: Calm, empathetic communication strengthens relationships and builds trust.

3. Productive Dialogue: A calm and understanding approach promotes productive dialogue, focusing on solutions rather than blame.

4. Conflict Prevention: Diffusing tensions prevents conflicts from escalating, fostering a culture of open communication.

Mastering Calmness and Empathy

Mastering the art of diffusing tensions requires practice and self-awareness:

1. Reflect on Reactions: Regularly reflect on your reactions to conflicts and identify triggers that lead to emotional escalation.

2. Develop Coping Strategies: Develop a toolbox of coping strategies to manage emotions during conflicts.

3. Enhance Empathy: Practice perspective-taking and empathy-building exercises to enhance your ability to understand others.

4. Continuous Learning: Continuously seek to refine your conflict resolution skills, incorporating feedback and insights.

Creating Harmony through Calm and Empathetic Responses

Diffusing tensions through calmness and empathy is a skill that transforms conflicts into opportunities for connection, growth, and resolution. By responding with composed understanding, individuals not only prevent conflicts from escalating but also foster an environment where conflicts are managed constructively. Through mastering the power of calmness and empathy, individuals pave the way for harmonious interactions and collaborative resolutions that honor the richness of diverse perspectives.

Stepping Back to Find Clarity and Solutions

In the heat of conflict, taking a step back can be a valuable strategy for gaining perspective, defusing tension, and finding effective solutions. In this chapter, we explore the art of stepping back to navigate conflicts with a clear mind, foster open communication, and arrive at resolutions that address the root causes. By learning to detach emotionally, assess situations objectively, and collaboratively problem-solve, individuals can transform conflicts into opportunities for growth and harmony.

The Power of Stepping Back

Stepping back involves creating a psychological and emotional distance from the conflict, enabling individuals to approach it with greater objectivity and composure. This technique prevents immediate emotional reactions and facilitates thoughtful responses that prioritize understanding and resolution.

The Role of Emotional Detachment

Emotional detachment is a crucial element of stepping back:

1. Emotion Regulation: Detachment allows emotions to settle, preventing emotional escalation and fostering rational thinking.

2. Expanded Perspective: Emotional detachment broadens perspective, enabling a clearer understanding of the conflict's dynamics.

3. Reduced Defensiveness: Emotional detachment diminishes defensiveness, creating space for empathetic communication.

Cultivating Emotional Detachment

Cultivating emotional detachment involves several strategies:

1. Mindfulness Practices: Engage in mindfulness exercises to stay present and detached from overwhelming emotions.

2. Pause and Reflect: Before reacting, pause and reflect on the situation to prevent knee-jerk emotional responses.

3. Distraction Techniques: Engage in activities that divert your attention and help you regain emotional balance.

Assessing the Situation Objectively

Objective assessment is a critical component of stepping back:

1. Identify Triggers: Recognize triggers that may cloud your judgment and emotional state during conflicts.

2. Separate Facts from Interpretations: Differentiate between objective facts and subjective interpretations of the situation.

3. Consider Others' Perspectives: Step into the shoes of the other party to gain insight into their viewpoints and emotions.

Fostering Open Communication

Stepping back paves the way for open communication:

1. Create a Safe Space: Ensure that both parties feel safe expressing their thoughts and feelings without fear of judgment.

2. Active Listening: Listen actively to each other's perspectives, validating emotions and promoting understanding.

3. Non-Defensive Responses: Respond with non-defensive language that demonstrates your willingness to collaborate.

Collaborative Problem-Solving

Stepping back sets the stage for collaborative problem-solving:

1. Identify Underlying Issues: Dig deeper to identify the root causes and underlying issues contributing to the conflict.

2. Brainstorm Solutions: Generate a range of potential solutions without judgment or evaluation.

3. Evaluate Solutions: Assess the pros and cons of each solution to determine the most suitable course of action.

4. Agree on Action Steps: Collaboratively agree on a plan of action that addresses the conflict's root causes and satisfies both parties.

Stepping Back in Action

Consider a scenario where a couple is arguing about household responsibilities. Without stepping back, the argument might escalate into a blame game. By applying the technique, they take a break to cool down and reflect. During this time, they assess their individual triggers and perspectives. When they reconvene, they communicate their feelings and collaborate to find a solution that meets both their needs.

The Benefits of Stepping Back

Stepping back offers numerous benefits in conflict resolution:

1. Enhanced Objectivity: Objectively assessing the situation prevents biases and emotional reactions.

2. Informed Decision-Making: Stepping back informs decision-making by providing a clearer understanding of the conflict.

3. Conflict Prevention: Emotional detachment prevents conflicts from escalating, preserving relationships.

4. Effective Communication: Objective assessment promotes open communication that focuses on understanding.

Cultivating the Art of Stepping Back

Cultivating the art of stepping back requires practice and intention:

1. Self-Awareness: Recognize your emotional triggers and the moments when stepping back is necessary.

2. Mindfulness Training: Engage in mindfulness practices to develop emotional awareness and detachment.

3. Reflection and Learning: Regularly reflect on your conflict experiences and learn from them to refine your stepping back approach.

Empowering Resolution through Stepping Back

Stepping back is a powerful tool that empowers individuals to navigate conflicts with a clear mind, empathetic communication, and collaborative problem-solving. By cultivating emotional detachment, assessing situations objectively, and fostering open dialogue, individuals can transform conflicts into opportunities for growth and understanding. Through the art of stepping back, conflicts become stepping stones toward resolutions that honor diverse perspectives, foster harmony, and cultivate meaningful relationships.

Chapter 6: Effective Problem Solving
Identifying the Underlying Issues in Conflicts

Effective problem solving is at the heart of conflict resolution. In this chapter, we delve into the critical skill of identifying underlying issues that contribute to conflicts. By digging beneath the surface, understanding the root causes, and addressing fundamental concerns, individuals can pave the way for lasting solutions that heal relationships and prevent future conflicts.

The Complexity of Conflict Issues

Conflicts often present themselves as surface-level disagreements, but beneath the visible arguments lie deeper issues:

1. Hidden Concerns: Conflicts can mask underlying fears, insecurities, or unmet needs that fuel emotional reactions.

2. Unexpressed Expectations: Unspoken expectations can lead to frustration and resentment when not met.

3. Past Baggage: Historical events and unresolved past conflicts can contribute to current disputes.

Unpacking the Underlying Issues

Identifying underlying issues requires a thorough exploration:

1. Active Listening: Listen to each party's perspective to uncover their underlying concerns and emotions.

2. Ask Probing Questions: Encourage open dialogue by asking questions that delve deeper into the issues at hand.

3. Explore Emotional Triggers: Understand the emotions triggered by the conflict, which often signal underlying issues.

Common Types of Underlying Issues

1. Communication Breakdown: Misunderstandings, misinterpretations, and poor communication can be the root of conflicts.

2. Unmet Needs: Conflicts may stem from unfulfilled emotional, psychological, or practical needs.

3. Value Conflicts: Differences in values, beliefs, and priorities can lead to disputes.

4. Power Struggles: Conflicts might arise from issues related to control, dominance, or a lack of equality.

5. Ego and Identity: Clashes in ego, personal identity, and self-esteem can trigger conflicts.

Addressing Underlying Issues in Action

Imagine a workplace conflict between two team members over differing work styles. On the surface, it's about the approach to a project, but underlying issues might include the need for autonomy, differing expectations, and a power struggle. By addressing these deeper concerns, the team members uncover common ground and work towards a collaborative solution.

Benefits of Identifying Underlying Issues

1. Holistic Resolution: Addressing underlying issues leads to comprehensive and lasting solutions.

2. Relationship Healing: Tackling root causes fosters understanding and healing, enhancing relationships.

3. Preventing Future Conflicts: By addressing fundamental concerns, you reduce the likelihood of similar conflicts arising in the future.

Challenges in Identifying Underlying Issues

1. Emotional Barriers: Strong emotions can hinder the objective identification of underlying issues.

2. Lack of Self-Awareness: Individuals might not be aware of their own triggers and underlying concerns.

3. Resistance to Change: Uncovering deeper issues may require individuals to confront uncomfortable truths.

Techniques for Identifying Underlying Issues

1. Reflective Analysis: Encourage individuals to introspect and identify their own emotions and concerns.

2. Third-Party Perspective: Seek input from a neutral third party who can provide insights into the conflict.

3. Comparative Analysis: Compare the current conflict with past conflicts to identify recurring patterns.

4. Journaling: Writing down thoughts and emotions can help individuals uncover underlying issues.

Fostering Constructive Dialogue

1. Create a Safe Space: Ensure both parties feel safe sharing their underlying concerns without fear of judgment.

2. Encourage Honesty: Promote open and honest communication about deeper feelings and concerns.

3. Validate Emotions: Acknowledge the emotions expressed by both parties to create a conducive environment for understanding.

Conflict Transformation through Underlying Issue Resolution

Identifying and addressing underlying issues transforms conflicts from battles over surface-level concerns to opportunities for growth and understanding. By delving beneath the visible disagreements, individuals uncover the true causes and foster empathy. Through this transformation, conflicts become catalysts for healing, deepening relationships, and forging resolutions that resonate with the core needs of all parties involved.

Brainstorming Solutions Collaboratively

Collaborative problem solving is a cornerstone of conflict resolution. In this chapter, we explore the art of brainstorming solutions as a collective endeavor. By leveraging diverse perspectives, encouraging creativity, and fostering open communication, individuals can generate a range of innovative solutions that address conflicts at their core. Through collaborative brainstorming, conflicts are transformed into opportunities for cooperation, growth, and sustainable resolutions.

The Power of Collaborative Brainstorming

Collaborative brainstorming harnesses the collective wisdom of individuals:

1. Diverse Perspectives: Each participant brings a unique viewpoint, enriching the pool of potential solutions.

2. Shared Ownership: Collaboratively generated solutions are more likely to be embraced by all parties.

3. Innovative Thinking: Interaction with different ideas sparks creativity, leading to novel approaches.

Creating an Atmosphere for Collaborative Brainstorming

1. Open Communication: Establish an environment where all participants feel free to express their ideas without judgment.

2. Respectful Listening: Encourage attentive listening to ensure that every perspective is heard and valued.

3. Embrace Creativity: Foster an atmosphere that encourages out-of-the-box thinking and unconventional solutions.

4. Non-Defensive Responses: Respond without defensiveness to encourage a safe space for sharing ideas.

The Process of Collaborative Brainstorming

1. Problem Definition: Clearly define the conflict or issue that requires resolution, ensuring everyone understands the context.

2. Generate Ideas: Allow participants to share their ideas without evaluation or criticism.

3. Combine and Refine: Group similar ideas and refine them, combining strengths to create more comprehensive solutions.

4. Evaluate Pros and Cons: Assess the potential benefits and drawbacks of each solution to make informed decisions.

Benefits of Collaborative Brainstorming

1. Enhanced Solutions: The collective input results in more well-rounded and effective solutions.

2. Increased Buy-In: Participants are more likely to commit to solutions they've played a role in creating.

3. Improved Understanding: Brainstorming promotes understanding by encouraging open dialogue.

4. Strengthened Relationships: Collaboration fosters a sense of teamwork and mutual respect.

Challenges in Collaborative Brainstorming

1. Conflict of Ideas: Differing opinions might lead to tension or difficulty in reaching consensus.

2. Group Dynamics: Power dynamics or dominant voices can stifle contributions from quieter participants.

3. Limited Creativity: Overthinking or fear of criticism can hinder the flow of innovative ideas.

Techniques for Effective Collaborative Brainstorming

1. Round-Robin: Each participant shares an idea in a structured, cyclical manner.

2. Silent Brainstorming: Participants jot down ideas privately before sharing them with the group.

3. Nominal Group Technique: Participants individually generate ideas and then share them for group discussion.

4. Mind Mapping: Create visual diagrams that connect related ideas, fostering creative thinking.

Facilitating Collaborative Brainstorming

1. Moderator: Designate a neutral person to guide the brainstorming session and ensure everyone has a chance to contribute.

2. Time Management: Set clear time limits for each phase to keep the process focused and efficient.

3. Idea Recording: Document all ideas shared to review later and ensure no contributions are lost.

Turning Collaborative Brainstorming into Action

Imagine a family conflict about allocating household chores. Through collaborative brainstorming, family members generate a range of ideas, from rotating responsibilities to outsourcing tasks. They discuss the pros and cons of each suggestion, taking into account individual preferences and constraints. As a result, they collaboratively devise a chore system that's equitable and suits everyone's needs.

Maximizing Collaborative Brainstorming's Potential

1. Value Diversity: Embrace different viewpoints and encourage participants to contribute from their unique perspectives.

2. Empower Silence: Create space for introverted or shy individuals to express their ideas comfortably.

3. Build on Ideas: Encourage participants to build on each other's ideas to create synergistic solutions.

Collaborative Brainstorming: A Path to Resolution

Collaborative brainstorming transforms conflicts from battlegrounds into spaces for shared problem solving. By engaging in open dialogue, embracing diverse viewpoints, and fostering creativity, individuals tap into a wellspring of innovative solutions. Through collaboration, conflicts are reframed as opportunities for growth, understanding, and unity. Collaborative brainstorming sets the stage for resolutions that resonate deeply, reflecting the collective effort of all parties involved and ushering in a new era of cooperation and harmony.

Prioritizing and Evaluating Potential Solutions

Effective problem solving requires not only generating solutions but also discerning the most suitable ones. In this chapter, we explore the critical process of prioritizing and evaluating potential solutions. By considering feasibility, alignment with values, and the impact on relationships, individuals can make informed decisions that lead to resolutions addressing conflicts in meaningful and sustainable ways. Through careful evaluation, conflicts are transformed into opportunities for well-rounded solutions and constructive outcomes.

The Significance of Prioritization and Evaluation

1. Optimal Outcomes: Prioritizing and evaluating solutions lead to decisions that yield the best possible results.

2. Resource Allocation: Effective allocation of time, effort, and resources ensures the chosen solution's success.

3. Relationship Preservation: Careful evaluation prevents solutions that might harm relationships in the long run.

Factors in Prioritizing and Evaluating Solutions

1. Feasibility: Assess the practicality and viability of implementing each solution.

2. Alignment with Values: Consider whether proposed solutions align with personal values and principles.

3. Impact on Relationships: Evaluate how each solution might affect relationships and long-term interactions.

4. Sustainability: Prioritize solutions that are sustainable and contribute to long-term well-being.

5. Balancing Interests: Seek solutions that strike a balance between parties' interests and needs.

Assessing Feasibility

1. Resource Availability: Consider the availability of time, finances, and personnel required for each solution.

2. Skills and Expertise: Evaluate whether the necessary skills and expertise exist to implement the solution effectively.

3. Risk Assessment: Identify potential risks associated with each solution and their impact on outcomes.

Evaluating Alignment with Values

1. Ethical Considerations: Examine whether solutions uphold ethical standards and values.

2. Long-Term Impact: Reflect on whether solutions resonate with personal values and contribute to long-term goals.

3. Consistency: Prioritize solutions that are consistent with overarching values and principles.

Considering Impact on Relationships

1. Short-Term vs. Long-Term: Assess whether the short-term benefits of a solution might negatively affect relationships in the long run.

2. Mutual Benefit: Seek solutions that benefit all parties involved, fostering trust and cooperation.

3. Communication: Evaluate whether the chosen solution promotes open and honest communication.

Promoting Sustainability

1. Long-Term Viability: Select solutions that can be sustained over time without causing undue strain.

2. Adaptability: Prioritize solutions that can adapt to changing circumstances and needs.

3. Environment: Consider the environmental impact of the chosen solution, if applicable.

Challenges in Prioritization and Evaluation

1. Bias: Personal bias can influence the evaluation process and lead to skewed decisions.

2. Emotional Attachment: Emotional attachment to certain solutions might hinder objective evaluation.

3. Limited Information: Insufficient information can make it challenging to assess the feasibility of solutions accurately.

Techniques for Effective Prioritization and Evaluation

1. Pros and Cons Lists: Create lists outlining the benefits and drawbacks of each solution.

2. Cost-Benefit Analysis: Quantify the costs and benefits of each solution to make an informed decision.

3. Decision Matrix: Develop a decision matrix that assigns weights to different factors and scores each solution accordingly.

Facilitating Collaborative Evaluation

1. Group Discussion: Engage in open discussions where all parties provide input on the evaluation criteria.

2. Consensus Building: Strive for consensus by addressing concerns and refining the evaluation criteria together.

3. Third-Party Facilitator: Involve a neutral third party to guide the evaluation process and prevent biases.

Putting Prioritization and Evaluation into Practice

Imagine a team facing a conflict about the allocation of project resources. By evaluating potential solutions, they assess feasibility, alignment with their company's values, and the potential impact on team dynamics. They collectively decide on a solution that ensures optimal resource utilization, upholds their values of collaboration, and maintains a positive team atmosphere.

Balancing Complexity and Effectiveness

1. Holistic Perspective: View conflicts and solutions from a comprehensive perspective, considering multiple dimensions.

2. Iterative Process: The prioritization and evaluation process may require iteration as new information emerges.

3. Feedback Incorporation: Continuously seek feedback from relevant stakeholders to refine your evaluation criteria.

Transforming Conflicts through Prioritized Evaluation

Prioritizing and evaluating potential solutions empowers individuals to make thoughtful decisions that resolve conflicts effectively. By considering feasibility, alignment with values, impact on relationships, and sustainability, individuals ensure that chosen solutions reflect the best interests of all parties involved. Through this process, conflicts are elevated from challenges to opportunities for growth, understanding, and transformative resolutions that foster harmony and lasting change.

Implementing and Reviewing Conflict Resolution Strategies

Effective problem solving reaches its culmination when chosen solutions are put into action and their outcomes assessed. In this chapter, we delve into the crucial phases of implementing and reviewing conflict resolution strategies. By taking deliberate steps to execute solutions, monitoring progress, and adjusting approaches as needed, individuals can navigate conflicts to successful resolutions that foster growth, understanding, and sustainable change.

The Dynamics of Implementation and Review

1. Action and Accountability: Implementation transforms plans into tangible actions, while reviewing ensures accountability and adaptability.

2. Feedback Loop: The cycle of implementation and review allows for continuous improvement and optimization.

3. Long-Term Impact: Well-executed solutions create a lasting positive impact on relationships and environments.

Navigating Implementation Challenges

1. Resistance to Change: People may resist new solutions due to comfort with the status quo.

2. Unforeseen Obstacles: Unexpected challenges might arise during implementation, requiring flexibility and adaptation.

3. Lack of Clarity: Misunderstandings about roles, responsibilities, or procedures can hinder smooth execution.

Effective Implementation Strategies

1. Clear Communication: Ensure everyone involved understands their roles, responsibilities, and the steps involved in implementation.

2. Timely Execution: Establish a timeline for implementation to prevent delays and ensure timely progress.

3. Support and Resources: Provide the necessary resources and support to facilitate successful execution.

Monitoring and Reviewing Progress

1. Regular Check-Ins: Schedule periodic check-ins to assess progress, address concerns, and celebrate milestones.

2. Feedback Gathering: Solicit feedback from all parties involved to identify areas for improvement.

3. Measuring Success: Define success metrics and assess whether the chosen solution is achieving the desired outcomes.

Adaptation and Adjustment

1. Flexibility: Be open to adjusting the implementation plan based on changing circumstances and feedback.

2. Refinement: Use feedback to refine strategies and enhance their effectiveness over time.

3. Iterative Process: Implementation and review can involve multiple iterations to fine-tune approaches.

Putting Solutions into Action

Imagine a community conflict over noise disturbances. The chosen solution involves implementing quiet hours and distributing guidelines to residents. During implementation, regular check-ins occur to assess compliance and gather feedback. Adjustments are made based on feedback, resulting in improved adherence to quiet hours and reduced conflicts.

Benefits of Effective Implementation and Review

1. Sustainable Change: Well-implemented solutions lead to lasting changes in behavior and attitudes.

2. Conflict Prevention: Regular review prevents conflicts from resurfacing and helps catch potential issues early.

3. Relationship Building: Successful implementation builds trust and fosters positive relationships.

Challenges in Monitoring and Review

1. Lack of Resources: Limited resources might hinder the ability to gather comprehensive feedback.

2. Inadequate Feedback: Unreliable or biased feedback can lead to inaccurate assessments.

3. Resistance to Review: Individuals might resist review due to fear of judgment or criticism.

Techniques for Effective Monitoring and Review

1. Surveys and Questionnaires: Gather feedback through structured surveys to assess satisfaction and identify areas for improvement.

2. Focus Groups: Organize focus groups to facilitate in-depth discussions and capture diverse perspectives.

3. Regular Reporting: Develop regular progress reports to track implementation milestones and outcomes.

Facilitating Collaborative Review

1. Inclusive Approach: Include all relevant parties in the review process to ensure diverse viewpoints are considered.

2. Non-Judgmental Environment: Create an atmosphere where individuals feel safe sharing honest feedback without fear of reprisal.

3. Feedback Synthesis: Synthesize feedback from different sources to identify common trends and areas for improvement.

The Ongoing Journey of Conflict Resolution

1. Continuous Learning: Use each implementation and review cycle as an opportunity for growth and learning.

2. Adapting and Evolving: Embrace the need for adaptation and evolution as conflicts and circumstances change.

3. Collective Responsibility: Recognize that successful implementation and review are collaborative efforts that require commitment from all parties.

Elevating Conflict Resolution through Implementation and Review

The journey of effective problem solving culminates in the successful execution of solutions and the iterative process of review. By conscientiously implementing strategies, monitoring progress, and making necessary adjustments, individuals can turn resolutions into transformative actions. Through this dedication to action and reflection, conflicts are not only resolved but also provide opportunities for personal growth, enhanced relationships, and a deeper understanding of how to navigate future challenges. The implementation and review phase marks the culmination of a holistic conflict resolution journey that empowers individuals to foster positive change and lasting harmony.

Chapter 7: Empowerment through Boundaries
The Role of Boundaries in Conflict Prevention

Boundaries play a pivotal role in conflict prevention, setting the framework for healthy interactions and relationships. In this chapter, we explore the significance of establishing and respecting personal and interpersonal boundaries as a proactive approach to conflict resolution. By understanding the nature of boundaries, learning to communicate them effectively, and recognizing their impact on conflict prevention, individuals can create a harmonious environment that minimizes conflicts and fosters mutual respect.

Understanding the Essence of Boundaries

1. Personal Space: Boundaries define our personal space, both physically and emotionally, helping us establish a sense of self.

2. Healthy Relationships: Clear boundaries contribute to building healthy relationships based on mutual respect and understanding.

3. Self-Care: Boundaries enable self-care by delineating what is acceptable and respectful treatment from others.

Different Types of Boundaries

1. Physical Boundaries: Defining personal space and comfort zones to prevent physical discomfort or intrusion.

2. Emotional Boundaries: Protecting emotional well-being by communicating limits on what emotions and conversations are acceptable.

3. Intellectual Boundaries: Respecting differing opinions and avoiding intellectual domination in discussions.

4. Material Boundaries: Establishing guidelines for sharing and using personal possessions to prevent conflicts over ownership.

Setting and Communicating Personal Boundaries

1. Self-Reflection: Identify your comfort zones, values, and what you are willing to tolerate or not tolerate.

2. Open Communication: Clearly communicate your boundaries to others, emphasizing that they are about self-care and not rejection.

3. Consistency: Maintain consistency in enforcing your boundaries to prevent confusion or manipulation.

4. Flexibility: While firm boundaries are important, allow for flexibility when circumstances warrant it.

Recognizing Others' Boundaries

1. Respectful Observation: Pay attention to verbal and nonverbal cues that indicate others' boundaries.

2. Empathy: Put yourself in others' shoes to understand their need for boundaries and respect their wishes.

3. Open Dialogue: Encourage open conversations about boundaries to ensure mutual understanding.

The Preventive Power of Boundaries

1. Conflict Avoidance: Well-defined boundaries prevent situations that might lead to conflicts from arising.

2. Respectful Interactions: Respect for boundaries fosters respectful interactions, minimizing the potential for disagreements.

3. Emotional Regulation: Boundaries help regulate emotional responses by preventing overstepping and triggering negative reactions.

Challenges in Boundary Establishment

1. Fear of Rejection: People might fear that setting boundaries will lead to rejection or conflict.

2. Cultural Differences: Different cultures have varying views on boundaries, leading to misunderstandings.

3. Assertiveness: Some individuals might struggle with assertively communicating and maintaining their boundaries.

Techniques for Effective Boundary Management

1. Self-Awareness: Continuously assess your own comfort zones and emotional well-being.

2. Direct Communication: Clearly express your boundaries using "I" statements and direct language.

3. Negotiation: In cases where boundaries might conflict, negotiate a middle ground that respects everyone's needs.

Facilitating Mutual Respect for Boundaries

1. Modeling: Set an example by respecting others' boundaries, encouraging them to reciprocate.

2. Educational Conversations: Educate others about the importance of boundaries in maintaining healthy relationships.

3. Creating a Safe Space: Foster an environment where individuals feel safe discussing their boundaries.

Harnessing Empowerment through Boundaries

1. Personal Empowerment: Boundaries empower individuals to define their limits, priorities, and self-care.

2. Interpersonal Empowerment: Mutual respect for boundaries strengthens relationships and prevents conflicts.

3. Conflict Transformation: A foundation of strong boundaries transforms conflicts into opportunities for understanding and growth.

Applying Boundaries to Real-Life Situations

Consider a workplace scenario where a colleague consistently interrupts your work. By setting a boundary and politely communicating your need for uninterrupted focus, you prevent potential conflicts and foster a more respectful work environment.

Balancing Flexibility and Boundaries

1. Adapting Boundaries: Be open to adjusting boundaries as situations and relationships evolve.

2. Consistent Core Boundaries: While flexible, maintain core boundaries to ensure self-respect and well-being.

3. Negotiating Boundaries: When boundaries intersect, engage in open discussions to find common ground.

Empowering Conflict Prevention through Boundaries

Boundaries serve as powerful tools for conflict prevention, shaping interactions and relationships in ways that prioritize mutual respect and understanding. By recognizing the diverse forms boundaries take, communicating them effectively, and respecting others' limits, individuals create a harmonious environment that minimizes potential conflicts. Through this proactive approach, conflicts are transformed into opportunities for respectful coexistence, personal growth, and lasting harmony.

Setting and Communicating Personal Boundaries

Boundaries are the cornerstone of healthy relationships and conflict prevention. In this chapter, we delve into the essential process of setting and effectively communicating personal boundaries. By understanding the importance of boundaries, identifying your limits, and mastering the art of communication, individuals can navigate relationships with clarity, foster respect, and create an environment conducive to preventing conflicts and promoting personal well-being.

Understanding the Significance of Personal Boundaries

1. Defining Your Space: Boundaries establish a psychological and emotional space that defines who you are and what you stand for.

2. Respectful Relationships: Clear boundaries set the tone for respectful interactions, ensuring your needs are acknowledged.

3. Self-Care: Boundaries are self-care in action, preserving your mental, emotional, and physical well-being.

Identifying Your Boundaries

1. Reflective Self-Exploration: Take time to reflect on your comfort zones, triggers, and areas where you feel uncomfortable.

2. Core Values: Your boundaries often align with your core values and principles.

3. Prioritizing Well-Being: Identify situations that leave you feeling drained or uncomfortable and recognize the need for boundaries.

The Art of Communicating Boundaries

1. Clarity: Be clear and specific when communicating your boundaries to avoid ambiguity.

2. Using "I" Statements: Frame your boundaries using "I" statements to express your needs without sounding accusatory.

3. Non-Defensive Tone: Communicate your boundaries in a non-defensive and non-confrontational tone to encourage openness.

Strategies for Effective Boundary Communication

1. Choose the Right Time and Place: Select a conducive environment for discussing boundaries, free from distractions.

2. Use Active Listening: Listen to the other person's response and acknowledge their feelings while maintaining your stance.

3. Stay Open to Discussion: Be open to discussing the rationale behind your boundaries and seeking compromise if necessary.

4. Respectfully Decline: Politely decline activities that go against your boundaries, offering alternative suggestions when possible.

Overcoming Challenges in Boundary Communication

1. Fear of Conflict: The fear of upsetting others might deter you from expressing your boundaries.

2. Guilt and Obligation: Feelings of guilt or obligation might make you hesitant to enforce your boundaries.

3. Misunderstandings: Miscommunications might arise due to assumptions or misinterpretations of your boundaries.

Cultivating Assertiveness and Confidence

1. Value Your Needs: Recognize that your needs and comfort are just as important as others'.

2. Practice Self-Assertion: Regularly practice assertiveness techniques to build confidence in communicating boundaries.

3. Visualize Success: Imagine successful boundary communication scenarios to alleviate anxiety.

Navigating Different Types of Relationships

1. Personal Relationships: Clearly communicate your boundaries with close friends and family to foster understanding.

2. Professional Relationships: Setting boundaries in the workplace ensures a productive and respectful environment.

3. Online Interactions: Extend your boundaries to digital spaces by being mindful of your online interactions.

Recognizing Respectful Responses to Boundaries

1. Acknowledgment: A respectful response acknowledges your boundaries without attempting to challenge or breach them.

2. Adaptation: People who value your relationship will adapt to your boundaries rather than attempting to change your mind.

3. Appreciation: A sincere appreciation for your honesty and willingness to communicate boundaries fosters trust.

Applying Setting and Communicating Personal Boundaries to Real-Life Situations

Imagine a scenario where a friend consistently cancels plans last minute, causing inconvenience. By communicating your boundaries assertively yet kindly—expressing that consistent cancellations are not acceptable—you establish mutual respect and encourage them to value your time and commitment.

Balancing Compassion and Self-Care

1. Empathy: Understand that others might have their own boundaries and communicate yours empathetically.

2. Self-Compassion: Prioritize your well-being by setting and maintaining boundaries while respecting others'.

3. Learning from Experiences: Reflect on past experiences to refine your boundary-setting skills over time.

The Empowering Process of Setting and Communicating Boundaries

Setting and communicating personal boundaries is a transformative process that empowers individuals to take control of their relationships and well-being. By understanding the significance of boundaries, effectively expressing your limits, and navigating potential challenges, you foster an environment of mutual respect and understanding. Through this proactive approach, you prevent conflicts, nurture meaningful connections, and pave the way for a harmonious and empowered journey through life.

Respecting Others' Boundaries

Respecting the boundaries of others is a fundamental aspect of fostering healthy relationships and conflict prevention. In this chapter, we delve into the art of recognizing, understanding, and honoring the boundaries set by individuals. By cultivating empathy, practicing active listening, and navigating the complexities of diverse boundaries, individuals can create an environment of mutual respect, trust, and collaboration that minimizes conflicts and nurtures harmonious interactions.

Understanding the Essence of Respecting Boundaries

1. Mutual Respect: Respecting others' boundaries demonstrates consideration, empathy, and a commitment to healthy interactions.

2. Building Trust: Honoring boundaries builds trust and establishes a foundation of respect in relationships.

3. Conflict Prevention: Respecting boundaries proactively prevents conflicts by avoiding situations that might trigger disagreements.

Recognizing Different Types of Boundaries

1. Physical Boundaries: Respect for personal space and comfort zones minimizes potential discomfort.

2. Emotional Boundaries: Acknowledging others' emotional limits fosters understanding and empathy.

3. Intellectual Boundaries: Valuing diverse opinions and perspectives prevents intellectual clashes.

4. Material Boundaries: Respecting possessions and belongings minimizes conflicts over ownership.

Practicing Empathetic Boundary Recognition

1. Empathetic Perspective-Taking: Put yourself in others' shoes to understand their need for boundaries.

2. Active Observation: Pay attention to verbal and nonverbal cues that indicate others' boundaries.

3. Open Communication: Encourage open dialogue about boundaries to foster mutual understanding.

Navigating Challenging Situations

1. Mismatched Boundaries: When your boundaries differ from someone else's, navigate with sensitivity and empathy.

2. Boundary Violations: Address boundary violations with care and understanding, offering space for discussion.

3. Cultural Considerations: Respect cultural differences in boundaries, recognizing that norms vary.

Applying Active Listening to Boundary Recognition

1. Attentive Listening: Listen actively to what others communicate explicitly and implicitly about their boundaries.

2. Non-Judgmental Attitude: Approach boundary discussions without judgment, promoting open dialogue.

3. Clarifying Questions: Ask clarifying questions to ensure you fully understand the boundaries being expressed.

Acknowledging the Freedom of Choice

1. Respecting Autonomy: Acknowledge that each individual has the right to set their own boundaries.

2. Non-Coercion: Avoid pressuring or coercing others to bend their boundaries to suit your needs.

3. Boundary Negotiation: In collaborative relationships, engage in open discussions to find middle ground.

Navigating Cross-Cultural Boundaries

1. Cultural Awareness: Educate yourself about cultural norms and expectations regarding boundaries.

2. Open Conversations: If in doubt, have open conversations about cross-cultural boundaries to avoid misunderstandings.

3. Adapting Gracefully: Adapt your behavior in a respectful manner when interacting with individuals from different cultural backgrounds.

Navigating Online Boundaries

1. **Digital Etiquette:** Practice digital etiquette by respecting online boundaries and privacy.

2. Consent and Sharing: Obtain consent before sharing others' information online, whether it's personal or professional.

3. Understanding Digital Boundaries: Recognize that digital spaces also have boundaries that deserve respect.

The Ripple Effect of Respecting Boundaries

1. Enhanced Relationships: Respecting boundaries nurtures positive relationships built on trust and understanding.

2. Conflict Minimization: Mutual respect for boundaries prevents potential conflicts and misunderstandings.

3. Empowerment: A culture of boundary respect empowers individuals to express themselves freely and confidently.

Applying Respect for Others' Boundaries to Real-Life Situations

Imagine a scenario where a colleague consistently works late and prefers not to be contacted after office hours. By acknowledging their boundaries and refraining from reaching out during those times, you demonstrate respect for their personal space and promote a healthy work-life balance.

Balancing Empathy and Boundaries

1. Empathetic Responses: Respond to others' boundaries with empathy, acknowledging their feelings and needs.

2. Open Dialogue: Foster open conversations about boundaries to promote mutual understanding.

3. Personal Growth: Respecting others' boundaries cultivates personal growth in understanding and empathy.

Respecting Boundaries: A Path to Lasting Harmony

Respecting others' boundaries is a transformative practice that enriches relationships, fosters empathy, and prevents conflicts. By recognizing diverse boundaries, practicing active listening, and navigating cultural nuances, individuals contribute to an environment of mutual respect and understanding. Through this commitment to honoring others' limits, conflicts are minimized, and opportunities for meaningful connections and collaborative interactions are maximized. Respecting boundaries is not just a practice; it's a mindset that contributes to the ongoing journey of harmony and personal growth.

Finding Balance between Flexibility and Boundaries

Balancing flexibility and boundaries is a delicate art that contributes to harmonious relationships and effective conflict resolution. In this chapter, we delve into the intricacies of maintaining a dynamic equilibrium between honoring personal boundaries and adapting to changing circumstances. By understanding the benefits of flexibility, recognizing when to uphold boundaries, and navigating the challenges of finding this balance, individuals can create a supportive environment that promotes growth, prevents conflicts, and nurtures resilient connections.

The Interplay of Flexibility and Boundaries

1. Dynamic Nature: Recognize that both flexibility and boundaries are essential for adapting to diverse situations.

2. Fluidity in Relationships: Healthy relationships require the ability to adapt while respecting individual limits.

3. Empowerment in Choice: Balancing flexibility and boundaries empowers individuals to make informed choices.

Benefits of Flexibility

1. Adaptability: Flexibility allows for adjustments in response to changing circumstances.

2. Open-Mindedness: A flexible approach encourages openness to new ideas and perspectives.

3. Conflict Prevention: Flexibility can defuse potential conflicts by accommodating differing viewpoints.

Benefits of Boundaries

1. Self-Respect: Boundaries affirm your self-worth by ensuring your needs and comfort are acknowledged.

2. Clarity: Boundaries provide clear guidelines for acceptable behavior, preventing misunderstandings.

3. Healthy Relationships: Respecting boundaries fosters mutual respect and prevents exploitation.

Navigating Situations Requiring Flexibility

1. Compromising for the Greater Good: Flexibility might involve compromising your personal preferences for a collective benefit.

2. Recognizing Changing Needs: Be attentive to shifts in circumstances that warrant adjustments to existing boundaries.

3. Assessing Long-Term Goals: Consider whether temporary flexibility aligns with your long-term values and objectives.

Recognizing the Boundaries to Uphold

1. Core Values: Identify the boundaries that align with your core values and principles, which should remain firm.

2. Non-Negotiables: Determine boundaries that are non-negotiable based on personal comfort and well-being.

3. Situational Boundaries: Some boundaries can be adapted depending on the context without compromising your values.

Challenges in Balancing Flexibility and Boundaries

1. Guilt and Obligation: Feeling guilty about setting boundaries might lead to excessive flexibility.

2. Overstepping Comfort Zones: Being too flexible can lead to discomfort and stress if personal boundaries are repeatedly crossed.

3. Fear of Conflict: The fear of conflict might deter you from enforcing your boundaries when needed.

The Fine Line of Adaptation

1. Situational Assessment: Evaluate whether the situation warrants flexibility or demands upholding personal boundaries.

2. Strategic Flexibility: Exercise flexibility strategically, recognizing when it aligns with your goals and values.

3. Communication: Transparently communicate your decisions to adapt or uphold boundaries to prevent misunderstandings.

Strategies for Balancing Flexibility and Boundaries

1. Mindful Decision-Making: Before making a decision, consider how it aligns with your boundaries and the potential impact.

2. Prioritization: Rank your boundaries based on importance to make informed decisions when flexibility is required.

3. Self-Check: Regularly reflect on your choices and assess whether they align with your values and comfort zones.

Creating a Supportive Environment

1. Respecting Others' Needs: Show understanding and empathy when others request flexibility due to their boundaries.

2. Open Communication: Encourage open conversations about balancing flexibility and boundaries in relationships.

3. Seeking Consensus: In situations involving multiple parties, work collaboratively to find a balance that respects everyone's boundaries.

Applying the Balance in Real-Life Scenarios

Consider a family vacation planning process where various family members have different preferences and needs. Balancing flexibility might involve adjusting the itinerary to accommodate everyone's comfort zones while upholding boundaries by ensuring that activities respect core values.

Building Resilience Through Flexibility and Boundaries

1. Adaptation as Growth: Flexibility and boundaries contribute to personal growth and resilience in navigating challenges.

2. Conflict Prevention: A balanced approach minimizes conflicts and misunderstandings.

3. Strengthening Relationships: Balanced flexibility fosters relationships built on trust, empathy, and mutual understanding.

Challenges in Flexibility and Boundary Balance

1. Pressure to Conform: External pressures might tempt you to compromise your boundaries excessively.

2. Striking the Right Balance: Balancing flexibility and boundaries can be complex and require ongoing adjustments.

3. Misinterpretation: Others might misinterpret your actions, assuming you are either inflexible or lacking boundaries.

Techniques for Practicing Flexibility and Boundary Balance

1. Daily Reflection: Reflect on your interactions and decisions, evaluating whether you balanced flexibility and boundaries effectively.

2. Seeking Feedback: Encourage trusted individuals to provide feedback on your balance between flexibility and boundaries.

3. Learning from Mistakes: Embrace mistakes as learning opportunities, adjusting your approach based on outcomes.

Promoting Collective Empowerment

1. Leading by Example: Demonstrate a balanced approach to others, inspiring them to prioritize both flexibility and boundaries.

2. Educational Initiatives: Educate your community about the importance of flexibility and boundaries in promoting harmony.

3. Supportive Discussions: Foster an environment where open discussions about flexibility and boundaries are encouraged.

Achieving Harmony through Flexibility and Boundaries

Striking a balance between flexibility and boundaries is a transformative journey that empowers individuals to navigate relationships and conflicts with resilience and understanding. By embracing the benefits of both, recognizing when to adapt or uphold boundaries, and navigating the challenges thoughtfully, individuals can create environments that promote mutual respect, growth, and lasting connections. This delicate equilibrium empowers individuals to prevent conflicts, nurture meaningful relationships, and lead lives characterized by empowerment, harmony, and personal fulfillment.

Conclusion

Reflecting on Your Conflict Resolution Journey

As you reach the culmination of this exploration into conflict resolution strategies, it's an opportune moment to reflect on the profound insights and transformative skills you've acquired. This final chapter invites you to look back on your journey through the foundations of conflict resolution, recognizing the growth you've undergone, and understanding how the principles you've learned can be integrated into your daily life. By pausing to reflect, you solidify your understanding, cement your progress, and prepare yourself for a future of harmonious relationships and empowered conflict resolution.

The Evolution of Your Understanding

1. Awareness of Importance: Recall the initial stages of your journey when you recognized the significance of conflict resolution in maintaining healthy relationships and fostering personal well-being.

2. Expanding Horizons: Reflect on how your understanding deepened as you delved into the various aspects of conflicts, communication, empathy, and self-awareness.

3. Embracing Empowerment: Consider how you've transitioned from feeling overwhelmed by conflicts to

embracing the empowerment that comes with proactive resolution strategies.

Applying Foundational Concepts

1. Conflict Recognition: Reflect on instances where you've now become more adept at identifying the signs of conflict, even in subtle forms.

2. Active Listening: Revisit conversations where you've practiced active listening, truly absorbing the perspectives of others.

3. Boundaries in Action: Recall moments when you set and respected boundaries, safeguarding your well-being and nurturing respectful interactions.

4. Empathy and Perspective-Taking: Think about times when you intentionally put yourself in others' shoes, bridging gaps in understanding and reducing misunderstandings.

5. De-Escalation Techniques: Reflect on instances where you've successfully prevented escalations, diffusing tensions through calmness and understanding.

6. Problem Solving: Revisit situations where you applied problem-solving techniques, addressing underlying issues and collaboratively brainstorming solutions.

7. Self-Awareness and Mindfulness: Consider moments when you engaged in self-awareness practices and

mindfulness, contributing to emotional intelligence and conflict prevention.

Growth and Learning

1. Lessons from Challenges: Reflect on challenges you encountered along the way and the valuable lessons they imparted.

2. Expanded Emotional Resilience: Recognize how your emotional resilience has expanded, allowing you to navigate conflicts with composure and understanding.

3. Empowerment Through Practice: Consider how your increasing proficiency in conflict resolution techniques has empowered you to navigate a diverse range of situations.

Incorporating Learning into Life

1. Personal Relationships: Reflect on how your understanding has influenced your interactions with family, friends, and loved ones.

2. Professional Context: Consider how you've applied conflict resolution principles in your workplace, fostering a harmonious and productive environment.

3. Community and Society: Reflect on the potential ripple effects of your improved conflict resolution skills on your community and society at large.

Challenges and Growth Ahead

1. Continuous Learning: Acknowledge that your conflict resolution journey is ongoing, and there's always more to learn and refine.

2. Adapting Strategies: Reflect on how you can adapt these strategies as circumstances evolve and relationships change.

3. Overcoming Setbacks: Consider challenges you may face in applying these techniques and how you can overcome them with resilience.

The Ongoing Path to Mastery

1. Commitment to Growth: Recognize that mastering conflict resolution is an ongoing commitment to growth, understanding, and compassion.

2. Embracing Complexity: Reflect on your readiness to embrace the complexities of conflicts and relationships as opportunities for growth.

3. Impact on Your Life: Consider how integrating conflict resolution strategies can impact your personal well-being, relationships, and overall life satisfaction.

Your Legacy of Empowered Conflict Resolution

1. Inspiring Others: Reflect on the potential to inspire those around you to embrace conflict resolution as a path to empowerment.

2. Contributing to Harmony: Consider how your commitment to these principles can contribute to a more harmonious world, one interaction at a time.

3. Continuing the Journey: Reflect on the exciting prospect of continuing your journey, exploring deeper levels of understanding and mastery.

The End Is Just a Beginning

As this book concludes, remember that your journey in conflict resolution is far from over. The insights you've gained, the skills you've honed, and the growth you've experienced are just the beginning of a lifelong quest to navigate conflicts with empathy, understanding, and empowerment. The wisdom you've acquired will serve as a guiding light, illuminating the path toward harmonious relationships and transformative conflict resolution for the rest of your life. The road ahead is paved with opportunity, growth, and the unwavering knowledge that you possess the tools to shape your interactions and the world around you for the better.

Applying Foundational Principles in Real-Life Situations

As you come to the close of this comprehensive exploration into conflict resolution strategies, it's time to bridge the gap between theory and practice. This final chapter emphasizes the practical application of the foundational principles you've learned throughout this journey. By applying these principles in various real-life scenarios, you not only solidify your understanding but also empower yourself to navigate conflicts constructively, cultivate harmonious relationships, and become a catalyst for positive change.

The Bridge from Theory to Reality

1. Bringing Concepts to Life: Reflect on how the theoretical knowledge you've acquired can be translated into practical actions in your everyday interactions.

2. The Power of Application: Understand that the true value of learning lies in the application of principles to create meaningful outcomes.

3. Personal Growth: Recognize how the act of applying principles is a catalyst for personal growth and transformation.

Applying Conflict Recognition

1. Everyday Conflicts: Identify small conflicts that arise in daily life and practice recognizing their underlying causes.

2. Preventive Measures: Consider how conflict recognition can help you identify potential conflicts early, allowing for timely resolution.

3. Conflict Prevention: Reflect on situations where recognizing conflicts helped you proactively prevent escalations.

Practicing Effective Communication

1. Conversational Dynamics: Apply active listening and constructive expression techniques to conversations with friends, family, and colleagues.

2. Resolving Misunderstandings: Consider how effective communication can clarify misunderstandings and restore harmony.

3. Empathetic Engagement: Reflect on moments when your empathetic communication defused tense situations.

Navigating Self-Awareness and Emotional Intelligence

1. Unveiling Triggers: Apply self-awareness to identify triggers that might lead to conflicts and consider strategies to manage them.

2. Emotional Regulation: Reflect on times when emotional intelligence helped you maintain composure during heated discussions.

3. Cultivating Empathy: Practice empathy and perspective-taking in real-time interactions, building bridges of understanding.

De-Escalation Techniques in Action

1. Preventing Escalation: Recall instances where you successfully applied de-escalation techniques to prevent conflicts from intensifying.

2. Diffusing Tensions: Reflect on how your ability to remain calm and understanding diffused tense situations.

3. Stepping Back Strategically: Consider how taking a step back to gain clarity enabled you to find effective solutions.

Effective Problem Solving in Real Scenarios

1. Collaborative Brainstorming: Apply collaborative problem-solving techniques to real-life challenges within your relationships and workplace.

2. Prioritization and Evaluation: Reflect on situations where you effectively identified and ranked potential solutions.

3. Implementing Solutions: Consider how implementing chosen solutions led to resolution and improved dynamics.

Empowerment through Boundaries in Practice

1. Respecting Others' Limits: Apply empathy when respecting others' boundaries, enhancing your relationships' harmony.

2. Setting and Communicating Boundaries: Reflect on instances where setting and communicating boundaries positively influenced your interactions.

3. Balancing Flexibility: Consider how you've balanced flexibility and boundaries in real-life situations, fostering understanding.

Guiding Principles in Real-Life Situations

1. Personal Relationships: Apply the principles learned to navigate conflicts within family, friendships, and intimate relationships.

2. Professional Context: Reflect on how these principles enhance your approach to conflicts and collaborations in your workplace.

3. Community Engagement: Consider the potential impact of applying these principles to community interactions and social engagements.

Challenges and Lessons from Application

1. Overcoming Setbacks: Reflect on challenges faced when applying these principles and how you overcame them.

2. Growth through Mistakes: Understand how learning from mistakes enhances your conflict resolution skills.

3. Adapting Strategies: Consider instances where you've adapted strategies to suit different situations and personalities.

The Endless Journey of Application

1. Lifelong Learning: Embrace the fact that applying these principles is a lifelong journey of growth and refinement.

2. Embracing Complexity: Reflect on your readiness to navigate the complexity of real-life situations with empathy and understanding.

3. Continuous Improvement: Consider how continued application and refinement will lead to increasingly successful conflict resolutions.

Empowering Yourself and Others

1. Leading by Example: Reflect on how your consistent application of conflict resolution principles can inspire others.

2. Promoting Positive Change: Consider the broader impact of your actions on the people around you and the communities you're a part of.

3. Contributing to Harmony: Understand that the principles you've internalized contribute to fostering harmony on both personal and societal levels.

The Beginning of a New Chapter

As this book concludes, remember that your journey is just beginning. The application of these foundational principles marks the initiation of a dynamic path toward personal transformation, enriched relationships, and empowered conflict resolution. Your capacity to understand, empathize, and communicate effectively equips you with the tools to create lasting change. The process of applying these principles, learning from experiences, and refining your skills is a journey of growth and empowerment that promises a future characterized by harmony, understanding, and the unyielding commitment to being a catalyst for positive change.

The Ongoing Path to Mastering Conflict Resolution

As you approach the conclusion of this comprehensive exploration into conflict resolution strategies, it's essential to recognize that this journey is not confined to the pages of this book. Instead, it is a lifelong endeavor, an ongoing quest for mastery that holds the potential to transform not only your interactions but also your entire outlook on relationships and the world around you. This final chapter delves into the nuances of the ongoing journey toward mastering conflict resolution, providing insights, guidance, and inspiration to continue honing your skills and fostering a life enriched with empathy, understanding, and harmony.

Embracing the Journey of Mastery

1. Beyond the Book: Understand that the knowledge you've gained is a foundation upon which you will build a lifetime of practical application and growth.

2. Constant Evolution: Embrace the notion that mastery is a continuous process of refining your skills, expanding your insights, and adapting to new challenges.

3. Empowered Living: Recognize that mastering conflict resolution is not merely a skillset, but a way of living that empowers you to navigate relationships with grace and understanding.

The Nature of Lifelong Learning

1. Curiosity and Growth: Cultivate a mindset of curiosity that drives you to seek new perspectives, ideas, and approaches to conflict resolution.

2. Learning from Every Interaction: Acknowledge that every interaction, whether positive or challenging, offers an opportunity to learn and improve.

3. Embracing Diversity: Embrace the diversity of human experiences and use them as opportunities to broaden your understanding of conflict dynamics.

Nurturing Emotional Intelligence

1. Continued Self-Awareness: Commit to ongoing self-awareness practices that help you identify triggers, emotions, and reactions.

2. Fine-Tuning Empathy: Understand that empathy is a skill that can always be honed, allowing you to connect more deeply with others' experiences.

3. Adaptive Emotional Regulation: Refine your ability to manage emotions in different contexts, enhancing your composure and effective communication.

Building Profound Communication

1. Advanced Active Listening: Elevate your active listening skills by tuning into subtler cues and underlying emotions in conversations.

2. Nuanced Expression: Work on expressing your thoughts and feelings with greater precision and sensitivity, ensuring clearer communication.

3. Mastering Non-Verbal Communication: Continuously refine your ability to interpret and use non-verbal cues, enhancing your ability to connect.

Navigating Complex Conflicts

1. Advanced Conflict Recognition: Sharpen your ability to identify conflicts even in intricate or subtle situations, preventing escalations.

2. Tackling Multi-Faceted Conflicts: Develop strategies for handling conflicts with multiple layers, considering diverse perspectives and needs.

3. Conflict Transformation: Explore techniques for transforming conflicts into opportunities for growth, collaboration, and understanding.

The Role of Wisdom in Mastery

1. Drawing from Experience: Understand that mastery is also rooted in accumulated experience, learning from past successes and challenges.

2. Wisdom in Decision-Making: Apply wisdom gained through practice to make informed decisions in complex conflict situations.

3. Long-Term Impacts: Reflect on the long-term impact of your conflict resolution skills on relationships, communities, and broader societal harmony.

Leading Through Example

1. Inspirational Impact: Recognize the influence your mastery of conflict resolution can have on inspiring others to adopt these principles.

2. Creating a Ripple Effect: Understand that your commitment to mastering these skills contributes to creating a ripple effect of empathy and understanding.

3. Contributing to Change: Embrace your role as a change agent, actively promoting a more harmonious and compassionate world.

Staying Resilient in the Journey

1. Embracing Challenges: View challenges as opportunities for growth and development, knowing that they contribute to your mastery.

2. Learning from Setbacks: Understand that setbacks are valuable learning experiences that can refine your skills and perspective.

3. Self-Compassion: Cultivate self-compassion, allowing yourself to learn and improve without excessive self-criticism.

Celebrating Progress and Growth

1. Personal Milestones: Reflect on the progress you've made on your journey toward mastery, celebrating each step forward.

2. Transformative Growth: Consider the personal transformation you've undergone, not just in your conflict resolution skills but in your overall character.

3. A Life Enriched: Embrace the enriched relationships, increased understanding, and positive impact you've created in your life.

Continuing the Journey Beyond

1. Lifelong Commitment: Understand that the journey of mastering conflict resolution is one that transcends time, weaving through the tapestry of your life.

2. Personal Legacy: Consider how your commitment to mastery will leave a legacy of empathy, understanding, and positive change.

3. A Fulfilling Path: Reflect on the fulfillment that arises from investing in the mastery of a skill that has the potential to influence countless lives.

A New Beginning with Every Interaction

As this book concludes, remember that every interaction, every conversation, and every conflict presents a new opportunity to apply and refine the principles you've learned. The ongoing journey of mastering conflict resolution is a testament to your commitment to personal growth, empathy, and understanding. Embrace each moment as a chance to contribute to a world where conflicts are transformed into opportunities for connection and growth. The path you've embarked upon leads to a life of enriched relationships, empowered communication, and a legacy of positive change. With every interaction, you create a new beginning—a chance to embody the principles of conflict resolution and continue your journey toward mastery with purpose, resilience, and an unwavering dedication to a harmonious and empathetic world.

THE END

Wordbook

Welcome to the glossary section of this book. Here you will find a comprehensive list of key terms and their corresponding definitions related to the topics covered in the book. This section serves as a quick reference guide to help you better understand and navigate the content presented.

1. Conflict Resolution: The process of addressing and settling disagreements, disputes, or conflicts between individuals or groups to achieve a peaceful and constructive resolution.

2. De-Escalation: Techniques and strategies aimed at preventing conflicts from intensifying or escalating further, often involving calming measures, communication, and understanding.

3. Empathy: The ability to understand and share the feelings, thoughts, and perspectives of others, allowing for a deeper connection and insight into their experiences.

4. Active Listening: A communication technique that involves genuinely concentrating, understanding, and responding to what the speaker is saying, promoting effective understanding and rapport.

5. Effective Communication: The skill of conveying thoughts, feelings, and information clearly and respectfully,

reducing misunderstandings and fostering constructive interactions.

6. Perspective-Taking: The practice of placing oneself in another person's position to understand their point of view and feelings, enhancing empathy and facilitating conflict resolution.

7. Compromise: A resolution strategy where individuals or parties reach a middle ground by making concessions and finding solutions that partially satisfy the needs and desires of all parties.

8. Win-Win Solution: An outcome in conflict resolution where all parties involved benefit or achieve their goals, ensuring mutual satisfaction and positive results.

9. Problem Solving: The systematic process of identifying, analyzing, and resolving issues or challenges to find effective solutions that address the root causes of conflicts.

10. Self-Awareness: A deep understanding of one's emotions, triggers, strengths, and weaknesses, enabling better emotional regulation and conflict management.

11. Boundaries: Personal limits, guidelines, or principles that individuals establish to protect their well-being, values, and comfort in various situations.

12. Conflict Triggers: Events, situations, or behaviors that initiate or exacerbate conflicts by evoking strong emotional responses in individuals or groups.

13. Empowerment: The process of equipping individuals with the knowledge, skills, and confidence to take control of conflicts, manage relationships, and make positive decisions.

14. Emotional Intelligence: The ability to recognize, understand, manage, and utilize emotions effectively in oneself and others, contributing to improved communication and conflict resolution.

15. Communication Styles: Different ways individuals express themselves and interpret information during interactions, influencing the dynamics of conflicts and resolutions.

16. Mindfulness: The practice of being fully present in the moment, allowing individuals to respond to conflicts with awareness and intention rather than react impulsively.

17. Negotiation: The process of discussion and compromise between parties with conflicting interests, aiming to reach an agreement or resolution.

18. Perception: The way individuals interpret and make sense of information, experiences, and situations, which can influence the course and resolution of conflicts.

19. Collaboration: Working together with others to achieve a common goal, often involving sharing ideas, resources, and efforts to find solutions.

20. Conflict Escalation: The process by which conflicts become more intense, adversarial, or volatile over time, often leading to more significant challenges in resolution.

Supplementary Materials

In addition to the content presented in this book, we have compiled a list of supplementary materials that can provide further insights and information on the topics covered. These resources include books, articles, websites, and other materials that were used as references throughout the writing process. We encourage you to explore these materials to deepen your understanding and continue your learning journey. Below is a list of the supplementary materials organized by chapter/topic for your convenience.

Introduction

Thomas, K. W., & Kilmann, R. H. (1974). Thomas-Kilmann conflict mode instrument. Tuxedo, NY: Xicom.

Folger, J. P., Poole, M. S., & Stutman, R. K. (2013). Working through conflict: Strategies for relationships, groups, and organizations. Pearson.

Pruitt, D. G., & Rubin, J. Z. (1986). Social conflict: Escalation, stalemate, and settlement. Random House.

Johnson, D. W., & Johnson, R. T. (2008). Social interdependence theory and cooperative learning: The teacher's role in the creation of positive interdependence and individual accountability. The Elements of Cooperative Learning, 2, 11-29.

Chapter 1: Nature of Conflicts

Deutsch, M. (1973). The resolution of conflict: Constructive and destructive processes. Yale University Press.

Wilmot, W. W., & Hocker, J. L. (2018). Interpersonal conflict. McGraw-Hill Education.

Pruitt, D. G., & Kim, S. H. (2004). Social conflict: Escalation, stalemate, and settlement (3rd ed.). McGraw-Hill.

Montada, L., & Kals, E. (2007). Culture, conflict, and conflict resolution. European Journal of Social Psychology, 37(2), 235-248.

Chapter 2: Effective Communication

Bolton, R. (2005). People skills: How to assert yourself, listen to others, and resolve conflicts. Simon and Schuster.

Beebe, S. A., Beebe, S. J., & Redmond, M. V. (2017). Interpersonal communication: Relating to others. Pearson.

Goleman, D. (2006). Emotional intelligence: Why it can matter more than IQ. Bantam.

Fisher, R., Ury, W., & Patton, B. (2011). Getting to yes: Negotiating agreement without giving in. Penguin.

Chapter 3: Self-Awareness in Conflict

Goleman, D. (1995). Emotional intelligence: Why it can matter more than IQ. Bantam Books.

Brackett, M. A., Rivers, S. E., & Salovey, P. (2011). Emotional intelligence: Implications for personal, social, academic, and workplace success. Social and Personality Psychology Compass, 5(1), 88-103.

Salovey, P., & Mayer, J. D. (1990). Emotional intelligence. Imagination, Cognition and Personality, 9(3), 185-211.

Brown, K. W., & Ryan, R. M. (2003). The benefits of being present: Mindfulness and its role in psychological well-being. Journal of Personality and Social Psychology, 84(4), 822-848.

Chapter 4: Empathy and Perspective-Taking

Davis, M. H. (1983). Measuring individual differences in empathy: Evidence for a multidimensional approach. Journal of Personality and Social Psychology, 44(1), 113-126.

Batson, C. D. (1991). The altruism question: Toward a social-psychological answer. Lawrence Erlbaum Associates.

Decety, J., & Jackson, P. L. (2004). The functional architecture of human empathy. Behavioral and Cognitive Neuroscience Reviews, 3(2), 71-100.

Chapter 5: De-Escalation Techniques

Pruitt, D. G., & Rubin, J. Z. (1986). Social conflict: Escalation, stalemate, and settlement. Random House.

Furlong, G. T. (2016). The conflict resolution toolbox: Models and maps for analyzing, diagnosing, and resolving conflict. John Wiley & Sons.

Ury, W. (2007). The power of listening in negotiation. Negotiation Journal, 23(4), 379-382.

Chapter 6: Effective Problem Solving

Fisher, R., Ury, W., & Patton, B. (2011). Getting to yes: Negotiating agreement without giving in. Penguin.

Daniels, A. C. (1999). Bringing out the best in people: How to enjoy helping others excel. McGraw-Hill.

Diver, S., & Shapiro, D. L. (2010). Conflict resolution across cultures. Journal of International Business Studies, 41(6), 935-955.

Chapter 7: Empowerment through Boundaries

Cloud, H., & Townsend, J. (1992). Boundaries: When to say yes, how to say no to take control of your life. Zondervan.

Adams, B. N., & Ineson, E. M. (2016). Respecting others' boundaries: An empirical examination of social constraints and ethical boundary perceptions. Journal of Business Ethics, 138(2), 227-243.

Conclusion

Neumann, C. S., Schmitt, D. S., Carter, R., Embley, I., Harenski, K., & Klapoetke, K. (2015). Are negative and positive parenting behaviors compatible? African Journal of Psychology, 45(2), 124-128.

Kuhn, T. S. (2012). The structure of scientific revolutions. University of Chicago press.

www.ingramcontent.com/pod-product-compliance
Lightning Source LLC
LaVergne TN
LVHW012106070526
838202LV00056B/5642